AN ORDINARY MAN,
an extraordinary life

Dr MALCOLM LINSELL

NEW
HOLLAND

Dr Malcolm D. Linsell
BSc, MBBS, MS, FRACS

The purpose of life is not to be happy. It is to be useful, to be honourable, to be compassionate, to have it make some difference that you have lived and lived well.
– Ralph Waldo Emerson

The best people possess a feeling for beauty, the courage to take risks, the discipline to tell the truth, the capacity for sacrifice. Ironically their virtues make them vulnerable: they are often wounded, sometimes destroyed.
– Ernest Hemmingway

For my parents, Frank and Jean Linsell, who taught me that my life is at its richest when I am focusing on others.

CONTENTS

Foreword

I don't remember much when I first came to Australia as I was three years of age at the time. Coming to Australia was a lifesaving journey for me.

There have been many operations, many hours put in to me, a lot of physical exercises and much more I don't even remember. Most of my earlier years, when I think about it, is only memories of pain and bucket loads of tears.

When I first met Malcolm I didn't like him because every time I saw him I knew there was going be some kind of pain involved with this guy. I hated him for that, no lie. I didn't like the way he would make me lift my head, stretch my arms, stretch my mouth and one thing I hated the most was wearing this cast that made my arms stay out that looked like I was doing the letter Y for the whole day. That was a pain in the ass.

As the years went by and I got older my fear of Malcolm eased, but not by that much! At this point in time I thought to myself, this guy is all right.

After going through getting burnt and then coming to Australia it was like everything hitting you at once and was very scary. Then to meet Malcolm and getting poked, probed and cut, but in the end of it all, even when I was very young I knew deep down this guy cared enough to put his time and effort into me. I always knew Malcolm was there to help me no matter how annoying and frustrating the process was.

Malcolm isn't just a friend or someone you occasionally talk to. He is a part of the Koni family. Things would have been a whole lot different if it wasn't for someone like Malcolm to take on such a challenge that was presented to him.

There are no words to express how grateful I am for what he has done in my life and the impact he has on my family and friends.

When we met a couple of years ago, for the first time in years, it was really good to see Malcolm; catching up with him, having a beer together and just chatting. To have the experience of us going together with Channel 9, back to my home country and village to show him where I came from was just amazing. It was a special moment when the helicopter landed and my dad came up to Malcolm and recognised him even after all those years.

I don't see Malcolm Linsell as my surgeon anymore, he is my family.

Cheers mate.

Wesley Koni

Introduction

When I first saw Wesley Koni, I was shocked. He was cradled in his father's arms, arriving in Melbourne, Australia late at night, having flown all the way from Onamuga in the Eastern Highlands Provence of Papua New Guinea (PNG). Photographs had given me some idea of his appearance, however, I was not prepared for just how deformed he was. Birth certificates in the PNG highlands are rare and although nobody really knew, he was estimated to be three or four years of age. His face appeared to be literally melted to his chest so that his head was rotated 90 degrees to his body. What would have been his right ear was attached to his right shoulder, his right eyebrow was attached in the vicinity of his right nipple and the right corner of his mouth near what would have been his left nipple.

My first thought was: What the heck am I going to do here?

It was 1993, I was 39 and only in my second year of plastic surgical practice. My medical and plastic surgical training had been of the highest standard. I had been privileged to work with some of the greatest clinicians and skilled surgeons of my generation in both Australia and the United Kingdom, yet nothing could have fully prepared me for the task I now faced.

I had been told that without surgical intervention, Wesley would die. For a young surgeon, I felt an enormous responsibility. Yet, this is what I had trained for. At the core of my being, is a desire to make a difference and to inspire others. It was one of the reasons I had done medicine and had became a surgeon. Here was an opportunity to use the skill that had been passed down to me through generations of surgeons, to make a real difference in the life of Wesley and his family.

This is the story of how I came to meet Wesley that night and how his story and mine have been inextricably linked over the ensuing 22 years. His is a story of courage and triumph in spite of horrific external deformity. Wesley is truly inspiring.

Mine is a story of an ordinary man being privileged to live an extraordinary life. I am honoured to share it with you and the important life lessons I've learned along the way.

Part One

Seemingly Insignificant Events Shape My Future

Cecil

Cecil Linsell, who preferred to be called 'Jack', was born in Romford Essex, in 1892. When still a lad, he was first attracted to the Salvation Army, which had commenced its work in the East End of London in 1865. At the age of 18, following the tragic death of his mother, Cecil boarded the *SS Otway* in London for its maiden voyage to Sydney, working on the ship to pay for his trip. He settled in St Peters, just to the south of Sydney and again became acquainted with the Salvation Army. In 1914, he entered the Salvation Army training college and a year later became a Salvation Army Officer. Ten years later, he met and married Letitia, an intelligent former schoolteacher who had also become a Salvation Army Officer. They had four children, the second of which they named Frank John Linsell.

After a time in Western Australia, the Linsell family settled in Adelaide where Cecil, now a Brigadier, managed the Whitmore

Square Men's Home, which was termed an 'oasis for the down-and-outers'. He was affectionately appointed a 'missionary' to the court where he consistently gave testimony on behalf of the men to whom he gave second, third and more chances. When he died of a heart attack in 1956 at the age of 64 (having had two previous heart attacks that he'd kept secret from his family) it was reported in the Adelaide papers that 'the lost, the lonely and the homeless will miss their most steadfast friend.' Others said that 'his weapons were patience, laughter, understanding and an unshakable faith in the people he was trying to help'. When news came through of his death, the court was adjourned and tributes flowed in from lawyers, judges and the men under his care. In an article in *The News*, headlined, 'The Deadbeats Have Lost a Pal', Brian Gill wrote that, 'His courage, the example he set, will live on to inspire his fellow workers in a wonderful cause.' His funeral is said to have stopped Adelaide. Whitmore Square Men's Home was later renamed Linsell Lodge. I am proud to say that Cecil Linsell was my grandfather and as a little boy I loved sitting on his knee and having fun. I now know that I inherited some of his characteristics.

Jean and Frank

My mother, Jean Ward, was born the youngest of three children in 1925. Her father was a blacksmith in the working class suburb of Footscray, Victoria. Although short in stature, he was a physically strong, loving man and as a small boy I thought he, my grandpa, made the best porridge in the world. Jean's childhood was tough and the family was poor. Whilst the circumstances are not clear, it appears Jean's mother, my grandmother, left her husband for long periods of time and Jean helped to raise the family. It has only been in the last few years, that we discovered that unbeknown to Jean, her mother gave birth to another son.

With the outbreak of World War 2, Jean's brother, my uncle Stan was conscripted into the Australian Army, at the age of 18. In 1942, with hundreds of other young Australians, he set sail for Singapore to fight the Japanese Army. The ship landed in the port of Singapore around the same time that Singapore fell to the Japanese. Stan was captured off the boat by the Japanese and taken to Sandakan. My Uncle Stan was one of the Allied Prisoners of War who died on a death march. Jean idolised Stan. His death impacted her deeply and maintaining the family unit was always a high priority.

Born in 1929, my father, Frank Linsell was four years younger than Jean. Frank's early life was centred on the Salvation Army in Adelaide. He grew up with several mates who remained loyal to each other all their lives. In later years, when they got together, they would retell the same stories and laugh and laugh. They were fun times for all the family and Dad was at his best when relaxed and laughing with his mates.

Both Frank and Jean felt called by God to be Salvation Army officers. Jean graduated from the Salvation Army's Training College in Melbourne and after appointments in Western Australia, found herself in Northern Victoria responsible for the Army's work with young people. It was here that she met a brand new Lieutenant who had just been appointed to Red Cliffs, a small fruit-growing town in Northern Victoria. Frank and Jean married in January 1954. In order to marry, Jean took a demotion in rank. Frank became the head of the house, the family and the local Salvation Army Corps (Church). Mum was smart and taking a backward step would not have been easy for a fiercely independent woman. Yet she obeyed rules and fell in line with what was expected of her.

Mum went into labour in the afternoon of early December 1954. Dad dropped her off at the Red Cliffs hospital with the words 'I'll see you in the morning love'. Frank drove off to attend the Salvation Army brass band rehearsal. I can imagine Jean responding with 'I'll be right love', for I subsequently heard her repeat these words many, many times.

I entered the world in the early hours of the following morning. Ironically, about 30 years later I assisted with a few plastic surgical procedures at the Red Cliffs Hospital. We tracked down my own birth records and laughed when I read that my mother had 'refused all sedation'. Those words just about sum up my mum—courage and dogged determination. She subsequently told me that, as I was the first child, she wanted to know what natural childbirth felt like.

The Salvation Army's military-style structure cultivates obedience and loyalty.

It is not surprising therefore that honesty, integrity and trust were the pre-eminent values of our family, and for this I will always be indebted to Mum and Dad who loved their God and the 'Army'. Not once did I hear them question their Farewell Orders—received in the mail by all Australian Salvation Army officers every December. Farewell Orders meant that officers either remained in their current positions or relocated to another position within two months. Such moves resulted in our family living in eight different houses in three states of Australia before I'd turned 12.

This might explain why I have always found it easy to move houses, move states and even countries. I still love to travel and my passport is always at hand. A few years ago, I recall being at work in Sydney one Saturday around noon, having a video conference with some colleagues in Singapore. Then and there I decided to go to Singapore for the weekend, booked, went home to pack a few things and made the 5pm flight.

Boyhood

I was born into a world of God's will, uniforms, brass bands, other people first, obedience and guilt. As a small boy it was difficult to separate facts from opinion. Life, however, was simplified because I was expected to do as I was told, without question. If I didn't I had to accept the consequences. Sometimes the consequences were more than just emotionally painful. The leather strap at home was nicknamed 'Malcolm's Own' and both Mum and Dad used it frequently on my legs to further my education.

One of the things life has taught me is that sometimes the most unexpected, unwanted, or even painful events can lead to never before considered outcomes. My first such lesson occurred at the ripe old age of nine months in the kitchen at home. Mum was cooking lollies or sweets for the local fair and had stacked our wood-burning stove so that it produced its maximum heat. I must have thought Mum might need some help so, using a chair, I climbed up the stove and managed to put both hands on the hotplate. I suspect it was the blood curdling scream rather than the smell of burning flesh which alerted Mum to the fact that things were not as they should be. The local doctor did what he could and bandaged both hands. I suffered full thickness burns to the palms of both hands, which took months to heal and left me with permanent unsightly scars, which persist to this day. Years later it was these same scars, which led me to my profession and some understanding of what Wesley Koni had gone through and what he would continue to go through.

In the Salvation Army in the 1950s, its musical focus meant that from an early age young boys were taught to play brass instruments and young girls, the tambourine. At that time no girls were permitted in the band. From about the age of five, I was taught to play the cornet and this would shape my life for decades.

I am forever grateful to the men who freely gave of their time to teach me a musical instrument. I am comforted by the fact that in return I was able to teach them patience for that is what they surely needed while trying to teach someone who thought he was God's gift to the musical world.

My first teacher owned a Volkswagen Kombi van that doubled as our rehearsal room. Heaven knows what a passer-by must have thought walking past a truck from which emanated very strained sounds of 'Onward Christian Soldiers' punctuated by a man yelling out the fingering positions at the top of his voice. Nevertheless, I showed some natural talent, which progressed to my first solo performance at the age of seven. Dad had arranged for me to play for the first time at a Sunday School anniversary. He wanted me to play the simple hymn tune 'Tucker'. What I didn't know was that 'Tucker' was also the name of a famous and challenging Salvation Army cornet solo.

I practised very hard for my first solo performance. When the night came, Dad was compering the programme. When he announced that, 'Malcolm Linsell will now play the cornet solo …'Tucker', the audience roared with laughter. I had no idea why. Nevertheless, I played as best I could and received a rousing ovation. It was years later that I realised how Dad had set me up and he always found this extremely funny.

Following this first performance, I was subsequently privileged to perform both as a member of a Salvation Army brass band and in a solo capacity in various settings throughout Australia and the world for the next 25 years. I went on to play the real cornet solo 'Tucker' on many occasions and perhaps not surprisingly, it became one of my favourite pieces of music.

At the age of six I recall visiting the local doctor with Mum and came away from the appointment thinking, 'I am going to be a doctor one day'. I am not sure what inspired me. It is unlikely my six-year-old insight had truly altruistic motives behind this choice for I have a strong suspicion that even at this age I had a desire to be wealthy and I was convinced that doctors must be very rich. Our family on the other hand, comprising my mum and dad, younger brother, Derek, soon-to-be-born sister, Denise, and myself were poor. Whilst the Salvation Army provided a house the weekly income was minimal. With equal mixes of willpower and faith, Mum and Dad seemed to make the small number of dollars stretch further than they should, but luxuries were few and far between. Those that did come our way were usually courtesy of generous members of the congregation. I will never forget the excitement of unexpected extra Christmas presents, and perhaps it is this that later initiated the desire to contribute to others who are less fortunate.

Whatever the reason, I became obsessed with the desire to become a doctor. My favourite television show was *Ben Casey*—an early medical show featuring a brain surgeon. My favourite books featured the human body, and one of my favourite past times was anatomical dissections. When I visited my uncle's farm I would accompany him whilst he slaughtered a sheep so that I could dissect the heart and lungs. On one occasion, being eager to discover how the organs functioned, I blew into the windpipe of a set of lungs that were still warm from their previous attachment to a sheep. I was so fascinated to observe the lungs expand that I had not thought beyond what happens when I stopped blowing. When this occurred the natural elastic recoil of the lungs took over, emitting a mixture of blood, sputum, and sheep's breath into the back of my throat. Even for the most eager doctor to be, trust me, this is not a recommended past time. Thankfully in later years I was taught how to do mouth to mouth resuscitation more effectively. It does actually work better if you remove your mouth from the airway in order to allow the other party to exhale.

In my early childhood, we didn't have a TV, so I would go to bed early. Mum would read to me every night and I knew my favourite *Dennis the Menace* book off by heart. When Dad would read, thinking I was asleep, he would skip a few pages, which would usually wake me up enough to admonish him and make him start again. School was fun and I loved learning. In grade one, I remember the whole class receiving their first book to read. I loved it and a few days later, surprised my teacher by waiting back after class to ask for the next book to read. I loved this time in my life. My school education had begun and I was learning a musical instrument. My friends and I would play in the street until the street lights went on and we couldn't see each other anymore. It was a time when I felt free, with not a care in the world and when I felt that nothing was impossible.

At the end of my first school year Dad received Farewell Orders and we moved from Burnie, Tasmania to Leederville, Western Australia. I was initially put into grade two but the teachers felt I was already advanced and so was placed into grade three. Consequently, for the rest of my schooling, I always seemed to be the youngest person in my year.

Performing in front of others seemed to come naturally. One day in grade three, the teacher asked for volunteers to read in front of the class. Being a 'goody two shoes', my hand shot up, even though I felt that my bladder was just a tiny bit full. In front of the whole class, I commenced reading only to realise my bladder was in fact full to capacity and no amount of leg crossing could prevent me from inevitably wetting my pants in front of the whole class. This indeed happened and as a pool was developing at my feet, the teacher graciously suggested I might be better to go to the toilet rather than complete the reading. I rather sheepishly followed her advice and rushed outside to the toilet.

I idolised my dad. He was fun, clever and seemed to be liked by all. Dad played basketball with the church team and I played in the junior team. At seven years of age I wanted Dad's number on the back of my basketball singlet, even though it was a number three and took much longer for Mum to sew the single piece of ribbon onto my singlet. I trusted him (and most others) completely. We usually went home together after basketball, however, one day, Dad had to stay on and asked a group of older boys from the church to walk me home. I was seven; they were about 14 and twice my size. About half way home, they decided to stop off at the church hall. Unbeknown to me, in a small room inside the hall, was a collection of discarded clothes that had been donated to the church. The boys disappeared into the room, locked the door and despite me banging on the door refused to let me in. I had no idea what was happening. I became afraid as I was left alone in a room for what seemed like ages and wasn't sure of my way home. I kept banging on the door, pleading with them to let me in. Suddenly, the door opened and they pulled me in, encircled me and seemed to tower over me. Each was dressed in old women's clothes and armed with broom handles. They were all laughing, menacingly. They forced me to the ground, held me down and in spite of my screaming, pulled down my shorts and underwear and used the broom handles to play with my genitals. My screams only seemed to make them laugh louder. When they had had enough they pushed me back into the larger room, slammed the door and continued to laugh. As a small boy I felt terrified, humiliated, ashamed and alone. I sat outside on the steps wondering what I could do. To go back in, risked it happening again; to find my way home seemed almost as scary. After what seemed a long time, I ran in the direction of what I thought was familiar and eventually found my way home. I didn't mention the incident to a soul and tried to shut it out of my memory. It wasn't until decades later that I realised that this was sexual assault. In the scheme of things, it is at the low end of assault, however, the abuse of power was very real.

The anger, hurt, shame and betrayal that I felt took some time and a lot of work to get over.

Abuse of any sort at any age is a violation of human dignity.

In spite of this, the early 1960s seemed an innocent time to grow up. My brother Derek and I were inseparable. When I was nine, my five-and-a-half-year-old brother and I would travel alone by bus to the football—rain, hail or shine. It didn't occur to us that we were poor. We each had sixpence to spend and this usually was spent on a packet of chewing gum, containing ten pellets. AFL has four quarters of football, which meant the ten pellets were spread out evenly over the course of the game. On the way home we would usually have all ten pellets in our mouth. That seemed like abundance to us.

On one occasion, the circus came to town and we wanted to attend. As we didn't have money to buy tickets, we needed to be creative. We waited until half-time and as the crowd was filing back in, we simply tagged along. Having no allocated seats, we decided to sit at ringside, which encouraged a few other children to do the same. Hence we got to watch the second half of the circus using no more than a little bit of boyhood ingenuity and cheek.

Being born into a moderately fundamentalist Christian family meant that God and faith played a pre-eminent role in my upbringing. From an early age I had a sense of something or someone greater than myself that I came to know as God, who to me, was inseparable from Jesus. In church we would sing a hymn called 'Only a Step to Jesus'. As a very young boy, I can remember taking big steps in the backyard of our home and getting quite frustrated with Jesus because He was not meeting me halfway.

Lying was not tolerated in our family. One day, Dad asked me to go to the shop to buy something. I said I would, however, I was thoroughly engrossed in what I was doing and forgot to go. Inevitably, some time later Dad asked how I had got on.

'I went but the shop was closed', I lied.

'Really?' said Dad. 'That's strange. Let's go and check.'

Knowing that I was in big trouble, reluctantly, I got in the car with him. Of course, the shop was still open and I muttered something like, 'They must have been cleaning behind the door,' compounding the lie. Dad knew I was lying. I knew Dad knew I was lying and I was banished to my room. The punishment was minimal yet this was an important lesson for me. Dad held me to account and exposed my lie. I don't recall ever lying to him again.

Tell the truth.

Another important lesson occurred around the age of ten and this time it challenged my budding entrepreneurial skills. The local retail store advertised a white basketball for sale for 13 shillings. I fell in love with this basketball and desperately wanted to purchase it. I was receiving one shilling (ten cents) per week as pocket money and I had worked out that this was just over three months to save the correct amount. To a ten-year-old, this seemed like an eternity, however, every week I would put my shilling into my piggy bank and count the weeks to go. After three months I had one week to go. Just one more shilling! That week was Sunday School anniversary and I was asked to give my testimony in Church as to the wonderful things Jesus was doing in my life. I saw an opportunity. I told my Sunday School teacher that I would give my testimony as long as he gave me one shilling. It seemed like a fair exchange to me. He would get what he wanted and I would get what I wanted. To my surprise he turned this generous offer down and I knew I was in big trouble when my father asked me about it on our way home from church. Again, I was banished to my room but that wasn't all. The next week, Dad called my Sunday School teacher and I into his room so that I could apologise for my dreadful behaviour. I have a sneaking suspicion that the two men had a laugh at my expense, however, for me it was hard to admit that I was wrong and that a better way of earning money, might not involve selling my services in church! Although it took a few more weeks to re-establish my pocket money cash flow, I eventually purchased the basketball and still have it to this day.

Do the right thing. Just because you can justify your behaviour, doesn't make it right.

Part Two

A Childhood Dream Becomes Reality

Puberty Blues

When I hit puberty at around the age of 13 I started to grow. You might think there is nothing strange in that, however, it caused me two problems. The first occurred with my hands because whilst normal skin is able to stretch with growth, scar tissue has no elastic properties and does not stretch. Consequently, the scar tissue in the palm of my right hand was pulling my fingers together. Functionally, the movement of my fingers was hindered and when buying items at the shop, I was embarrassed to receive change in my right hand. I felt abnormal and different to everybody else. My left hand was less scarred so I used this instead. So I have personal experience of how a physical deformity can have an emotional impact on the way people feel about themselves.

I needed an operation to release the burn scar contracture of my dominant right hand and for this I was referred to a well-respected plastic surgeon in Perth, Western Australia, Mr John Hanrahan.

I loved being in hospital and I was fascinated to be wheeled into the operating theatre for the procedure. I loved seeing all the equipment and was asking the anaesthetist questions as he put me off to sleep. Under general anaesthetic, the scar on my hand was incised to allow my fingers to be stretched out. This left a diamond shaped area of raw tissue in the palm of my hand measuring 4cm by 3cm. A full thickness skin graft was taken from my groin and carefully sewn onto my hand to cover the raw area. In order to limit movement and give the skin graft every chance of 'taking', my right hand was bandaged and placed in a plaster. As I was waking from the anaesthetic, I recall feeling very nauseous and the most relief I received for this was when a nurse sat with me and stroked my hair (yes, I did have some at the age of 13!). I will never forget that touch of kindness and it has had a direct impact on how I treat my patients. A simple touch at the right time (for both men and women) helps to allay fear and reassures patients that they are in the right hands and being cared for. Nowadays, operations such as this are often performed as day surgery. In those days, however, I was in hospital for almost a week. I got very used to being looked after by the nursing staff and was most disappointed when I was told that I had to go home.

The operation itself was extremely successful and I regained full use of my hand. One slight drawback is that full thickness skin carries hair follicles with it. Whilst my groin skin at 13 was hairless, as I got older I began to grow hair, which is normal for the groin but not for the palm! I am grateful when jokes about growing hair on the palm of my hand are kept to a minimum!

What happened next, was to have a major impact on my future. My sutures were removed from my hand and groin two weeks after the operation in Mr Hanrahan's room. I was standing outside the rooms waiting for Dad to pick me up, when Mr Hanrahan backed out of his driveway in a Jaguar and moved off down the road. As my eyes followed him, I clearly recall saying to myself 'I want to be like that man'. At the age of 13, I decided I was going to become a plastic surgeon. Twenty-five years later the same plastic surgeon became one of my examiners. Indeed, he failed me, twice, despite the fact we had paid his bill a quarter of a century earlier!

The other problem with growth was that I became fat. It would somehow seem easier to say this was due to a hormonal imbalance or my 'glands', but unfortunately it boiled down to the fact that I ate too much of the wrong types of food. I, however, had little insight into why I was fat and endured the humiliating self-consciousness of gynaecomastia (male breast tissue) and a big belly. At that time we were living in Perth, a beautiful city characterised by its warm and often hot weather. It was not unusual to finish school at 4pm then head down to the beach with my friends for an hour or so body surfing. I was fine in the water but because of my self-consciousness, I was usually the last to remove my shirt and the first to put it back on.

In my first year of high school, I recall a physical education teacher who insisted that all outdoor sporting activity for the boys be performed bare-chested. I pleaded with him to allow me to wear a singlet, but he refused with a smug look on his face and I could almost hear him think 'it serves you right for being fat!' Surrounded by my friends and peers the humiliation was intense, not just because I was self-conscious of my appearance, but also because of the frustration that existed because I didn't know why I was fat or if anything could be done about it. Nevertheless, I firmly believe in karma and not long after this incident happened the same teacher was displaying his basketball skills shooting for goal. I had perfected an underarm throw from the free-throw line that had served me well. He ridiculed this so I challenged him to a one on one competition with the winner to be the person throwing the most number of baskets. Sensing a major confrontation, dozens of kids gathered around to watch and in fact to cheer me on. It was quite possible I was motivated by revenge, for I can remember being absolutely determined to win. This I did, to the rousing cheers of my friends. The teacher disappeared quickly and never talked to me again. He was a bully. At the time I didn't feel particularly courageous, but standing up to him had the desired effect.

In 1968 I had just turned 13. I was fat, shy and very unsure of my place in the world. I had spent most of my childhood in Perth and the family had now been transferred to the large city of Melbourne, Victoria. Not long after we arrived, I attended a music camp and whilst we were waiting for everybody to arrive, the boys were playing a game of 'kick the kick' with an Australian Rules Football. I was quite good for my short stature and one of the observers was overheard to say, 'Who's the fat kid taking all the marks'? The observer turned out to be Graham McCoy, a good looking and talented musician who had a lot more success with girls than I did. Graham and I later became the best of friends, a friendship that has lasted to the current day.

The move to Melbourne meant I attended my fifth school in seven years and again I jumped a grade moving from first year high school in Perth to third form at Camberwell High School.

My recollections of Camberwell High are centred on particular teachers and students. I remember our music teacher Mr Travare being gifted, but eccentric. Eccentricity is also the best word I can find to describe Mr Wilkinson who liked to wear short sleeves in winter and jumpers in summer. There was Miss Rusden who portrayed a tough exterior, which I always suspected covered a heart of gold. And then there was Mrs Tempest. She was a beautiful woman who loved us all, yet somehow was able to make me feel unique and special. Teachers play a huge part in influencing our lives, for which they seem to receive little credit or financial reward.

I must, however, give a special mention to Mr Mitchell. When he wanted his class to give him their attention, he would call out 'eyes and ears'. We were expected to put down our pens, look to the front and listen intently. I thought I might put a slightly different interpretation on the saying. One day I brought to school two large plastic ears that had been lying dormant in the bottom of one of the cupboards at home. I gave one to my friend so that when the command for 'eyes and ears' was made, we would both lob an ear from the back of the classroom and aim to hit the blackboard. (It seemed funny at the time.) Unfortunately, we were both quite excitable youths. When the command was made we promptly stood up and hurled the ears with all the force we could muster. One of us, I can't remember which, had a particularly poor aim. Mr Mitchell who was sitting at his desk, was hit flush in the face with a large plastic ear, which sent his glasses flying across the desk. All but three people roared with laughter. Mr Mitchell was stunned more than anything else. My friend and I knew we were in deep trouble.

To his everlasting credit, Mr Mitchell gathered his thoughts, and his glasses, and asked the perpetrators to come forth. This we did and rather than march us straight to the principal's office, Mr Mitchell acknowledged the intent, but suggested that a more appropriate action would have been to simply get up and place the ears on his desk. In retrospect, that would have been just as funny and not put us at risk of an assault charge.

Whilst in third form I joined the school bounce ball team. This was no mean feat because most of the team consisted of fully-grown sixth formers and I was still struggling through puberty. Bounce ball is a game similar to volleyball, but played on a trampoline. I managed to make the team for the interschool grand final. After some torrid competition we won 16–2. (I lost the two games, but at least I won one game against an angry young man twice my size.)

In fourth form, I was one of four people selected to take part in a radio interview. I have no idea why I was selected and I had no idea about the subject of the interview, which had something to do with engineering. We went to the ABC studios in the city, microphones were put in place and an interviewer took us through a run through. I said absolutely nothing because, to me, it was as if they were speaking in a foreign language. I had no idea what they were talking about. As the rehearsal went on, the sound technician kept coming into the studio and moving the microphone away from me. At first he was quite subtle, however, by the time the actual interview took place, all microphones were pointed directly away from me. It was embarrassing and I have never been more relieved than when the interview completed and my only contribution had been a few grunts and some appropriately timed 'yeses'.

It became abundantly clear to me that I am not a person who can ad lib or talk when I know nothing about the subject. For me to do well, I need to prepare, rehearse and have at least some idea what I am talking about.

Around the age of 14, I fell in love for the first time. Fiona Boyd was very cute and sought after by other boys, so I felt very privileged that we would spend time together at school socials and occasionally after school. Sometimes I preferred spending time with her rather than attending my after-hours chemistry lessons that were scheduled at school. Taking Fiona out was not an option because the rule at home was that I had to be 16 before I could take any girl out. However, I do recall receiving a lift home from a school social accompanied by Fiona. My friend, who was 18 and drove the car, parked just down the road from my place. I was in the back seat with Fiona and the windows started to miraculously fog up. At one point I surfaced to see a flash of red outside the car door. It was then I realised it was my mother, in her red dressing gown, who had come out to check on me. I got the shock of my life. The sight of my mum, in her red dressing gown and slippers, could well be described as a major passion killer.

Musical Interludes

Every year, Camberwell High School held a choral festival. All school students were divided into one of four houses, with each house named after a famous international politician. I was appointed to Roosevelt House as was my brother Derek. All members of each house formed a choir and competed against each other at the choral festival. Conductors for the choirs were expected to train the often-unwilling students over a six-week period, and then conduct them during the performance in front of the whole school. Conductors volunteered. In form six—my final year of school—the selected set piece was the classic hymn, 'Jerusalem'. I thought I could conduct the Roosevelt House choir, however, I was still shy and held back from volunteering. Instead, a female friend of mine bravely put herself forward.

Rehearsals over the first two weeks were not going well so after a discussion between the two of us, she graciously handed over the role of conductor to me. This was the first time I had ever taken on a leadership role, where I was responsible for the performance of 150 people. It was daunting, for I knew precious little about choral singing, yet also exciting. Having by now, played cornet solos in front of audiences of hundreds of people, I was used to centre stage, however, this was about me talking, seeking to pass on a little bit of musical knowledge, whilst inspiring and motivating them to do their best. 'Jerusalem' starts with the line, 'And did those feet in ancient times...'. My brother still reminds me how embarrassed he was when, in my opening speech to the choir, emphasising the importance of diction, I said, 'I don't care what Anne did. I want to hear, 'AND DID those feet.' The choir seemed to respond to my enthusiasm and to my somewhat acrobatic conducting. We were fortunate to have a brilliant pianist named Michael Tyach accompanying us and together, on the day of competition, we were fortunate to win.

*People want to be led. If the goal is clear
and they feel it is worthwhile, people
will follow a leader they think will get
them there.*

I have fond memories of my involvement in and playing trumpet with the Camberwell High School dance band. Camberwell High School was a conservative school and I suspect that we were catalysts for breaking a few shackles.

I remember a time during rehearsals for the choral festival. As a conductor I, of course, was expected to be at all rehearsals, which were usually held during the recess period. On one occasion I was rehearsing with the dance band at the back of the new gymnasium. I was having such fun playing some new Joe Cocker songs that I completely lost track of the time. By the time I looked at my watch, I was already ten minutes late for choir rehearsal. This wouldn't have been so bad, but the McCarthur House choir were actually rehearsing in the gymnasium, so for me to get to my rehearsal I had to walk through the middle of the throng. I very sheepishly forced my way through the crowd whilst trying to reassure everyone that I had not been spying on them.

The highlight for the dance band was performing on the Australian talent TV show, *New Faces*. Because our rehearsals were generally within school hours, in order to prepare for the television appearance we were given the day off and we rehearsed all day. Anybody who has played a brass instrument will know that the longer one plays the more tired the lip muscles become. (This is a fact not often understood by guitarists who seem to be able to play all day without ill effect.) By the time we got to play in front of the cameras my lips felt like jelly. The sound that emanated from my trumpet was also very much like jelly hitting the floor! We played

Lead cornet of the Camberwell Salvation Army Band, aged about 16.

Family photo with my mum and dad, Frank and Jean Linsell. I was four years old and my brother Derek was still a baby.

My brother Derek and sister Denise seeing me off at Melbourne airport on my way to London in 1987.

Solid Rock on the back stage at Sunbury. I am in the back row, third from left.

My first degree, a Bachelor of Science from Monash University in 1975.

Above: A Masters of Surgery from Monash University. Left to right, Mum, Dad, myself, Fiona, Derek and Denise.

One of my favourite shots of Bek and Tim.

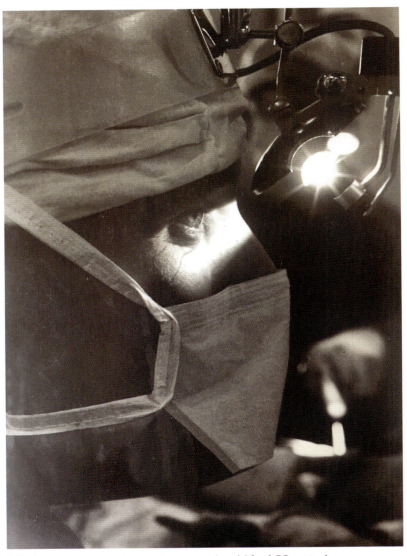

Working as a vascular registrar at the Alfred Hospital.

Dr Malcolm Linsell and Dr Kim Carr-Linsell, newly married.

Our four children, Tim, Indi, Mike and Bek.

The bridal couple. I look pretty happy because I am.

the Glenn Miller classic, 'In the Mood', however, the mood we put the judges in was not what we would have preferred. At least we thought we looked good in our school uniforms.

Because I showed some talent playing the cornet and trumpet, music was a major part of my life. I played the cornet in the Camberwell Salvation Army brass band, one of Australia's best Salvation Army bands and had moved on to playing more difficult solos. At the age of 14, the local Returned Serviceman's League asked me to play 'The Last Post' at the eleventh hour of the eleventh day of the eleventh month in 1968, the fiftieth anniversary of Armistice Day. 'The Last Post' is not technically difficult, however, I was perched on the wall of the post office at Camberwell Junction, one of the busiest road intersections in Melbourne. At 11am, the police stopped all traffic (there were no traffic lights at the intersection at that time) and in complete silence, I played 'The Last Post' waited for a minute, then finished with the Reveille. It was a profound experience to be given that honour at such a young age. The veterans were so pleased with the ceremony that they presented me with a hand painted certificate and photograph to commemorate the occasion. It was such an honour.

Based in London, the International Staff Band of the Salvation Army is internationally recognised as the pre-eminent brass band in the Salvation Army. Only the very best players are accepted into the band. An Australian named Brian Davies played cornet in the band for a few years before returning to Australia and accepting the position as bandmaster of the Camberwell Salvation Army. Brian was a naturally brilliant cornet player and he became my mentor for many years. A pharmacist by profession, he was smart and successful, both with his career and with his musical ability. Brian set high standards for me and inspired me to reach them. Because he was able to combine his professional career with his family life and still be one of the world's best cornet players in the Salvation Army, it was simply a matter of following his advice as he had already achieved goals that I wanted for myself. At 15, he appointed me to be the lead cornet player of the Camberwell band, a position I held for the next 18 years. The lead (or top chair) cornet player in a brass band has a similar role to a lead violin in an orchestra. It was my role to personally maintain a high standard of music and lead primarily by example. I was privileged to do this and play with the band in our local church, with numerous interstate visits throughout Australia and then international tours of New Zealand, USA, Germany, Sweden, Norway and Denmark along with two tours of the UK including an appearance at the Royal Albert Hall in London.

*The right mentor can lead you to where
you want to be.*

Around the same time I was taking on more responsibility with the band, I finally persuaded Mum and Dad that my 'puppy fat' was not going to disappear, so we paid a visit to the local doctor. In the late 1960s, expert nutritional knowledge was rare and my doctor was no exception. After searching through a pile of papers in the bottom of one of his drawers, he handed me my first diet. By this stage the discipline that was necessary for regular cornet practice and long hours of study had become ingrained so I followed the diet religiously. For lunch I ate soggy crisp bread and vegemite (which tasted more like wet cardboard) and I also began exercise with running, sit-ups and push-ups. I lost 12 kilograms in a month, initiating my passion for correct nutrition and exercise, which has lasted to this day. Not only did I look better, the change in the way I felt about myself was dramatic. I became less self-conscious and more confident and I have no doubt this was already laying the foundation for my future career. I resolved to never be fat again.

University…just

In my final year of secondary school when most others were enjoying themselves playing sport or socialising, I would rise early, study for an hour and practise my cornet for an hour before I went to school, then hit the books again after school until late at night. I was consumed with the desire to get enough marks to enter the medical faculty and at the same time be the best cornet player I could be. Consequently, I had little time for anything else. One day, I was at an older friend's place and was asked my opinion about something. I was shocked because I could not recall ever being asked for my opinion before and I didn't know what to say. The culture I knew, required me to 'do as I was told' without question. To this point in my life, my brain had been used for remembering facts and musical notes; the concept that I could create my own unique thoughts was as remote as an outback toilet. I also realised, the expression of an opinion opened the possibility that another would not like it, and by inference not like me. This created a dilemma for a teenager who was unsure of himself outside his protective environment.

I could not have worked harder as I prepared for my matriculation examinations. I drove myself to exhaustion and, in retrospect, my lack of downtime was a hindrance rather than a help. Yet working harder was all I knew at the time. Five written exams—each of three-hours' duration—fifteen hours of writing to determine the direction my life would take. As with all other students who have gone through a similar process, it felt very daunting for a shy, insecure 16-year-old with limited ability, yet a burning desire to do my best.

Months later, my examination results arrived by post. I locked myself in my bedroom to read them and was devastated to realise, that whilst they were above average, they were well below the cut-off point for entry into medicine. Furthermore, whilst I had been offered a place to study for a science degree at Monash University I had not received a scholarship to fund the university training. Given my parents lack of financial resources it appeared that I might not even be able to attend university. It was one of the lowest periods of my life because I was entirely focused on university and doing medicine and it appeared that I was not good enough to do either. I had little time to consider all of this by myself, for Mum and Dad were knocking at my door wanting to know my results. Whilst they were disappointed for me, to their credit they were fully supportive believing something would turn up. I wouldn't be surprised if, for the next few weeks, Mum spent quite a bit of time in prayer letting God know that He needed to sort things out. With only a few days remaining before university commenced, completely out of the blue, I was awarded a 'free place', which was a special scholarship for children of low-income earners. I had never heard of such a thing, yet it meant I could commence a Bachelor of Science degree at Monash University and all my tuition fees were fully paid for. Poverty rules!

I had not long turned 17 when I commenced University with the sole aim to get enough marks to transfer to medicine. For a boy who had lived a somewhat sheltered existence, had been told what to do and almost always obeyed the rules, University was an eye opening experience. From the images of naked women on the front cover of the University newspaper (complete with expletives), to the waft of marijuana smoke emanating from one of the cafeterias, to the lack of accountability for attending lectures. To me, this was a whole new and exciting world. Seemingly for the first time in my life, I was not obligated to do anything. Consequently, during first semester, I thought this was an ideal time to improve my game of snooker. Unfortunately, in the mid-year maths examination, knowledge of snooker was not a prerequisite and for the first time in my life, I failed an exam.

Clearly this was not an ideal preparation for getting the marks required to transfer to medicine. Thereafter, I became more diligent with my study and began to look on the biomedical library at Monash University as my second home. I had developed the art of power napping whilst studying and when tired I would nap for ten minutes, literally mid-sentence, then wake and continue reading the sentence. In this way, I could study for long periods without a long break.

When I sat the maths exam at the end of the year, I was prepared. When I later received my mark for the year, I was astonished to see that I had achieved a distinction for maths. In order to do this, I calculated that I must have received an almost perfect score for my final exam. The hard work was paying off. At the end of first year I applied for a transfer to medicine, however, the transfer was denied.

He's a Lumberjack and He's Okay!

One of the great things about university is the holidays between the end of one year and the commencement of the next. During one of these breaks, in true Monty Python form, I became a lumberjack! This came about because an older friend had shared with me about his logging project and how I could make a lot of money over the holidays by felling trees. In turn, I shared the money-making bonanza with my friends Graham McCoy and Chris Coates and we three budding entrepreneurs agreed to meet early the following Monday to travel to a forest north of Melbourne.

When Monday arrived, each of our cars was temporarily incapacitated however, after making a few frantic phone calls, we managed to borrow a car from a friend of a friend. This car was a Hillman circa 1960. None of us had any experience with such a car, however, in our enthusiasm to do a good job on our first day, we headed off for the 90-minute ride to the forest. About 45 minutes into the trip there was a loud snapping sound from under the bonnet and shortly thereafter, the car came to a stop. We were in the middle of nowhere. We lifted the bonnet and while our combined mechanical knowledge would fit on a postage stamp, even we could diagnose that the fan belt had snapped. It would be another ten years before mobile phones were introduced to Australia, so we could either flag down another car or find an alternative solution. We decided to walk to an adjacent farmhouse to seek help. An old farmer answered the door and after listening intently to our garbled explanation of our predicament, said that he just might be able to help. He took us to his garage, unlocked the door and to our utter amazement, there stood a Hillman car, the exact same make and model of our vehicle. Furthermore, he just happened to have a spare fanbelt that he was only too happy to give to us, free of charge.

On subsequent occasions, I have thought about the series of events that took place for that extraordinary 'coincidence' to take place. Was it just a coincidence or was there something (or someone) else at work? I don't profess to know the answer but I do know that Graham, Chris and I shared a unique experience together that helped to cement our friendship that has lasted more than 40 years. It seems to me that life is not just a series of random events that would happen anyway given enough time. There are times in my life where there seems to be an invisible, gentle force at work. It is a Spiritual presence that I know as God. It is hard to describe, as it is more a knowing that transcends rational thought and in my experience, God seems to have my best interests at heart. I have a belief that if my heart is aligned with correct principles and my intention is to do the right thing, things tend to work out for the best…sometimes better than I could have hoped. This might not be immediately apparent for there have been times of deep despair, however, I have found that resilience is a character trait that has allowed me to overcome difficulty, learn from the experience, and subsequently prosper.

There is a Spiritual dimension to life that transcends rational thought.

When we finally arrived at the forest, our spiritual enthusiasm was somewhat dampened as we took in the task before us. Our brief was to fell trees of a limited diameter, cut them into specific lengths, then carry them to the edge of the forest for later pick up and delivery to landscaping outlets. There were thousands of trees and not one of us had any experience with a chainsaw. I was elected chief chainsaw person and on the job I learned how to fell a tree in the general direction of where I wanted it to fall. Mostly, I got this right! There were only a few times when things didn't go to plan and a tree came crashing down within inches of one of my mates. In the hot sun of a Melbourne summer, the sweat poured off us as we lifted log after log and carried them to the edge of the forest. Chris had a saying he learned when conscripted to the regular army, namely, 'Thumb in bum and mind in neutral!' It was put to good use during this time. Physically, I have never worked harder and I would like to say this was all worthwhile because we made an abundance of cash. Unfortunately, this was not the case, however, there were three major benefits. Firstly, I have a deep respect for all those who have physically demanding jobs. Secondly, over a two-month period we developed chiselled bodies, honed to near perfection (well, that's what we thought), however, my love of ice-cream saw that disappear just as quickly. A career with Manpower was never an option. Thirdly, we laughed and laughed at ourselves and each other, sharing an experience that we all treasure. I have found that it is the sharing of experiences, with those I love, that have given me the most joy and contribute to the richness of life.

One of life's joys is sharing experiences
with those I love.

Blowing My Own Trumpet

The sound that emanates from a brass instrument is dependent on the embouchure of the lips and the mouthpiece of the instrument. A cornet mouthpiece is similar to that of a trumpet and if the tubing of both were stretched out, they are identical in length at a little more than a metre. Most cornet players can therefore play trumpet and vice versa. The difference is the sound. A cornet has a more mellow and sweeter sound (though I have heard some cornet sounds, particularly when I was practising, that would seriously challenge this). The trumpet sound is harsher and more 'brassy' in nature.

When I was invited by John Cleary (now a respected ABC presenter and commentator) to play trumpet in a big band comprising fellow members of the Salvation Army, I jumped at the opportunity. For the ultra-conservative Salvation Army in the 1970s, Solid Rock, as we came to be known, was a challenge for some and an exciting alternative for many. At that time, Salvation Army bandsman were required to only play music that had been approved by the Salvation Army Music Board. Solid Rock challenged that as a few of the band's extremely talented members, wrote their own charts, specifically for the band.

Solid Rock quickly gained a strong following with the younger generation and soon developed a broader appeal. We played to thousands of people both in Melbourne and interstate, recorded a couple of albums, appeared on radio and television shows including

Hey, Hey It's Saturday (where Daryl Somers had a guest gig on drums) and we played on the second stage of the Sunbury Pop Festival.

The Sunbury Pop Festival was Australia's answer to Woodstock. It ran from 1972 to 1975 and was held on a private farm near Sunbury in Victoria. It was a natural amphitheatre with a creek running through the valley. The stage was built at the bottom of the hill and attendees simply camped out in the open over the January Australia Day weekend. I attended most years, working with the Salvation Army in a tent pitched half way up the hill. For some, we seemed to provide the only non-alcoholic refreshment they had over the whole weekend. It was pretty hot, so swimming in the creek, usually without togs, was a favoured past time although observing from the riverbank seemed to be even more popular. To witness live performances from Billy Thorpe and the Aztecs, Queen, Skyhooks and Deep Purple to name a few, was a huge thrill. It was a unique experience for Solid Rock to appear at such a venue and in time the band became more accepted by Salvation Army leadership. Full credit goes to John Cleary, Ralph Hultgren, Brian Hogg, Barrie Gott and others for having the vision to see and plan for a future beyond the constraints of conservatism.

It takes vision and courage to move
beyond the status quo.

If At First You Don't Succeed…

After each year of my science degree, I applied for a transfer to medicine. Each year this was denied. By the end of 1974, I had completed my science degree, majoring in physiology and pharmacology, I was about to turn 20 and I had a major decision to make. I would soon be awarded a Bachelor of Science (BSc), however, medicine had been my solitary aim from the age of six. It appeared I was just not good enough to get in. Again I had applied for a transfer to medicine, however, I had received no reply and thought that all was lost.

I was invited by the science faculty to do an Honours year and I knew I could apply to medicine again once the Honours year completed, however, there were no guarantees I would be successful. I began to think that perhaps it was just not meant to be.

At the time, it therefore seemed logical to me to apply for pharmacy, which was a different, yet related course. My application to commence pharmacy was successful and I had mixed feelings. Should I give up on my dream of medicine, working intimately with people and making a difference or be practical and move on to a career which would be fulfilling and profitable, yet was a little more detached from people?

Reluctantly, I attended the first day of orientation into the pharmacy faculty. I just didn't want to be there. I was a conflicted individual, feeling grateful for the opportunity to be a pharmacist and yet sad that I was not going to become a doctor.

At the end of day one of pharmacy, I returned home somewhat dejected. I retrieved the mail from the letterbox and absent-mindedly flicked through the letters. Then I saw it. A letter addressed to me from the Faculty of Medicine, Monash University. Perhaps it was to officially inform me that again my application had been unsuccessful. Then again, it just might mean…

With trembling fingers, I opened the letter, which went something like this…

Dear Mr Linsell,

I have pleasure in informing you that you have been accepted to commence training in second year of the Faculty of Medicine. Please contact our office to arrange a time for you to meet the Dean.

Yours sincerely,
Secretary to the Dean
Faculty of Medicine
Monash University

These were the sweetest words I had ever read. I wept.

I was flooded with emotion; excitement, gratitude, humility, relief, fulfilment and joy. 19 years previously, as a toddler I had sustained a terrible accident leaving a permanent scar. As a six-year-old I had decided to be a doctor, then at 13 years of age, whilst benefitting from a doctor's skill, was inspired to be like him. This childhood dream was about to become a reality. I called Mum and Dad to share the news. They were ecstatic as we celebrated together. It was one of the happiest days of my life.

When a dream becomes a burning desire
and is coupled with hard work, the
Universe often conspires to transform the
dream into a reality.

Part Three
Training, Training and More Training

Bedside Manner

I was so excited to commence my medical training. At that time, the medical degree required six years of full-time study. I had been admitted into second year, which meant I had a further five years of university to go. The next two years were to be spent on the university campus while the final three would be centred in a hospital closer to the city of Melbourne. I didn't mind. I had just turned 20 and I loved every minute of the course. Whether it was in lectures learning about the normal development and function of the various compartments of the human body or looking down the microscope at histology slides, I found it fascinating. What I loved most was anatomy. We were privileged that each year, generous people donated their bodies to the university to enable us to learn. Some of the body parts became prosected specimens that were preserved in see-through containers, so we could follow the course of nerves or blood vessels from their origin through to the organs or muscles they were supplying.

Other bodies were preserved whole for medical students to dissect, so we could be hands on and get a feel for human tissue. I will never forget the experience of walking into the dissecting room for the first time. We all had to wear long white coats every time we entered the room so on day one, there were about 120 medical students dressed in their crisp white coats, talking excitedly as we waited outside the room. When the doors opened the first thing that struck me was the cold. The room was of course kept cool to preserve the bodies for a full 12 months. The next sensation was the smell. The bodies were preserved in formalin, which has a distinctive, pungent smell. The smell of formalin seems to seep into your clothes and skin and it is so heavy, it is as if you can taste it. That smell would be with me for the next two years.

Yet, nothing can really prepare you for the sight of the bodies themselves. Until that day, in second year medicine, I had not seen a dead body, so the sight of 20 naked cadavers—that not that long before had been living, breathing human beings—was quite confronting. The bodies were laid out on metal tables and scattered at regular intervals around a large room. There were seats around each of the tables and we all quite solemnly took a seat where we could. The room was cold, stark and pungent. For the next two years we would spend a good deal of our time in this room and before each session, one of the demonstrators gave a lecture from the front of the room focusing on the area we were to dissect. I am not sure how effective these lectures were. It seems to me that if full recall was the intention, it might be best to not to present information in a freezing room, with an overwhelming pungent odour surrounded by dead bodies.

We were divided into groups of six and an anatomy demonstrator was assigned to each group. The first region to dissect was the buttock.

None of our group wanted to go first so our demonstrator, Dr (now Professor) Jeffrey Kerr said he would make the first incision as long as it was the last one he would make on our behalf. As the incision was made, I was struck by how leathery and thick the skin appeared. (It was a few years later that I discovered that living skin behaves quite differently because of its elasticity and flexibility. Furthermore, the skin of the buttocks and back is the thickest skin of the whole body.) Soon the skin was peeled back revealing the underlying gluteus maximus muscle. I was fascinated and had soon overcome any misgivings, taking the scalpel to make my first incisions into human skin, albeit that of a dead person. The human body is a magnificent creation. It is stunning in it's intricacy at both micro and macroscopic levels. Even 40 years later, I am still fascinated by how the human body works and its ability to heal itself. After all, in order to treat patients, surgeons initially create injury to the skin and underlying tissues. We can only do what we do primarily because the body has remarkable methods of healing itself.

Around this time, I witnessed my first surgical procedure. At the time, the Salvation Army owned and ran the Bethesda Hospital in Melbourne. Dad arranged for me to attend an operating list performed by a plastic surgeon. My very first operation was, believe it or not, a breast augmentation (an operation I have subsequently personally performed hundreds of times). I remember thinking, 'You are going to put *that* in there?' Nevertheless, I loved every minute of it. The surgeon asked me what anatomy region I had been studying. When I told him it was the buttock, he asked me to describe it. I was so overawed, I couldn't remember a thing and I am sure my description of the path of the sciatic nerve bore no resemblance to reality.

When I reached fourth year in medicine, university life as I knew it changed forever. In second and third years we had learned about normal anatomy and function of the body. Armed with this knowledge, fourth-year medical students were physically relocated to teaching hospitals around Melbourne. I was fortunate enough to be allocated to the Alfred Hospital, one of Victoria's pre-eminent teaching facilities. At that time, Dad was working in the city and would brave the peak-hour traffic by driving, with his mates, by car each day. On most days I would hitch a ride with them, laughing along with the same stories until they dropped me off at the hospital.

Medical students were required to buy their own stethoscopes and white coats. (We had short white coats to separate us from the doctors who wore long white coats.) This was so exciting because I was getting closer to becoming a doctor. I still have my first stethoscope. The clinical school adjacent to the hospital housed our lectures as we now started to learn about sickness, disease and its treatment.

When a patient dies in hospital, often an autopsy is performed to determine the cause of death. As part of our training in Pathology, each morning we would gather in the Padua theatre, named after the first anatomical theatre built at the University of Padua in 1594. At the Alfred Hospital, it consisted of a central display area surrounded by tiers of semi-circular levels where we would stand and view the organs from the previous day's autopsies. These were delivered to the theatre in metal boxes about the size of a small suitcase and contained the heart, brain, lungs, liver, kidneys, major blood vessels and anything else that was of relevance to how the patient had died. This was initially quite confronting, however, I quickly got used to the gruesome reality and came to recognise the signs in the heart of a heart attack, or a stroke in the brain, or the black lungs and clogged blood vessels of a smoker, or the signs of cancer with its spread to other organs. This 'in your face' medical training has a sobering effect, highlighting the fragility of life and that all of us will one day end up in a similar situation.

*Life is precious. As far as I know we only
get one chance at it, so never take it
for granted.*

Patients in major teaching hospitals in Australia receive care that is of world-class standard. The surgeons, physicians and nurses are highly skilled and the fact that most patients receive the highest quality medical care at no cost to themselves, is a tribute to Australia's medical system. One of the drawbacks for such patients is that they can often be inundated with Medical Students. If a patient had a heart murmur, some crackles in their chest, an enlarged organ, a neurological disorder, an unusual disease or just a lump or bump, every medical student from years four to six, wanted to listen to their heart or lungs, palpate their abdomen, examine their nervous system or feel their lump. Some patients tolerated this well and were used to students, particularly if the students were respectful. Other patients got fed up (as one would expect) and displayed the dreaded 'No Students' sign above their bed.

As fourth-year students, we were divided into groups of about eight then assigned a consultant surgeon or physician who would take us to visit a patient they were often treating at the time. Our aim was to learn the art of taking a patient's history and examining them in order to reach a diagnosis. This can all be read in textbooks, however, actually talking to a real patient, asking the right questions in a systematic fashion to get accurate answers, then being able to communicate the history to a colleague in a meaningful way, is a skill all doctors must acquire. Medical students also have to learn a new language. It is the language used by doctors to communicate with each other and is vitally important particularly in an emergency situation. Unfortunately, doctors sometimes assume that patients understand this language, which, after the doctor has left, has patients asking nurses or even medical students to 'translate' for them. I recall learning about pseudopseudohypoparathyroidism (which is a rare medical condition) and was delighted to know that at that time it was the longest word in the English language.

Our groups of eight, with consultant in tow, would crowd around a patient's bed. One of us would elicit the history and then often all eight of us would examine the patient. This seems a fairly clumsy way to learn (and it is) however, thanks to some incredibly tolerant patients (and consultants) in time, we became more confident.

There is an apocryphal story among medical students that one consultant while teaching his students to listen and watch everything, took a little pot of patient's urine, dipped a finger in it, then put his finger in his mouth.

'Now do what I just did,' he said.

One by one, the horrified students dipped their fingers in the urine then tasted it.

'Now what did you learn?' he asked.

Like good students, each of them described the aroma and various taste sensations in great detail. They sounded like some wine drinkers do nowadays.

'Rubbish!' he exclaimed. 'That's not the point. None of you watched what I did. I put my index finger in the urine and put my middle finger in my mouth!'

The more time we spent on the wards, with patients, the better we got. Of course, there was also the added benefit of fraternising with the nurses. When I was doing my medical training, nursing training was all done from within the hospital as nurses learned on the job. This meant there was quite a strong connection between nursing students and medical students. I, of course, as one of my consultants used to say, had a lot of bad luck in that area and so I focused primarily on my studies!

Whilst I am on the subject, nurses are an amazing group of people. There are very few who do not have patient care as their main priority, and we all benefit from their selfless devotion to their patients. Nurses deal with illness and suffering and sometimes death, all day every day. They are constantly communicating with patients, family, doctors and allied medical staff often in stressful circumstances. In the wards, doctors might be present for a few minutes every day. For the rest of the 24 hours, it is the nurses who care for the patients. In the operating theatre, it is the nurses who make sure everything runs smoothly. They are managing both patients and doctors alike, often working long hours to provide the best possible care for their patients. The health care system would collapse without them. Doctors couldn't do the work they do, without nurses. I couldn't have done and continue to do, what I do, without the skill, expertise and caring of nurses. For the knowledge they have and for the work they do, they are grossly under recognised, under appreciated and underpaid.

Fame and wealth are poor barometers for
contribution to society.

India

Fifth year medicine included an elective where we could spend up to six weeks involved in something that would contribute to our medical career. I wanted to go to somewhere as remote as possible and chose to go to India. Through my Salvation Army contacts I arranged to spend time at the Catherine Booth Salvation Army hospital in Nagercoil, Tamil Nadu, about 24km from the southern tip of India. This was a life-changing experience.

My first impression was of the Indian people. They could be living in most abject poverty, or be suffering intensely, however, they always seemed to have a smile on their face and with a shake of their head, let me know that all was okay.

On my first night, I was guest of honour at the nurses' graduation ceremony. I was given the honour of handing out the certificates and I had some idea that the left hand was considered unclean because it is associated with going to the bathroom. I, of course, thought I was above thousands of years of Indian culture and proceeded to shake hands with my right and hand out the certificates with my left. The gasps of horror that escaped from the crowd gave me some indication this might not be a good idea. I hope the girls kept their certificates!

My next impression was of the operating theatre. In Australia I had seen a few operations performed in a sterile environment with the patient put to sleep by an anaesthetist, placing an injection of pentothal into the patient's vein then a tube down their windpipe to control their breathing, whilst they were asleep. In Nagercoil, pentothal was either unavailable or too expensive, so all general anaesthetics were performed using ether anaesthetic. The patient lay on the operating theatre, a wire mask like a vegetable strainer was placed over their nose and mouth, a rag placed on the mask and ether poured onto the rag. In breathing in the ether fumes, the patient was soon asleep and the anaesthetist could control the depth of anaesthesia by continuing to pour on more ether. With this highly efficient method, I saw some amazing and complex procedures performed.

In India, betel nut has been chewed for thousands of years. It is commonly kept in the mouth for extended periods of time to moisten the mouth in the hot Indian sun. One of the adverse effects is cancer of the mouth and face. Disfiguring tumours grow on the face, spread elsewhere through the body and kill people. Not long after I arrived, I witnessed an operation on a woman who had her entire cheek removed for cancer of the face caused by betel nut. Even nowadays reconstruction of this defect is a challenge because a thick, flexible piece of tissue is required, with skin on the facial surface and mucosa on the inside of the mouth. I watched in amazement as the surgeon used the patient's scalp to reconstruct the defect. The scalp was shaved, and a bi-lobed flap (similar to Mickey Mouse ears) was raised, still attached to its blood vessels, the raw surfaces folded on itself, then inserted into the face as a new cheek. Performed under ether anaesthetic, this was some surgery! When this type of surgery works well, hair continues to grow in the transplanted tissue. I can imagine this woman shaving the outside of her cheek, however, shaving the inside of her mouth might have been a little more problematic.

Every morning, I would do a ward round with the American surgeon who was spending time at the hospital. A member of the Salvation Army, he was a Christian gentleman and I will never forget visiting the patients whose cancers were already beyond operating or cure. The surgeon would spend time with each and every one, touch them (even those with leprosy) and pray with them. Often the patients were Hindu and spoke no English, however, the gratitude of the patients and their families was immeasurable. This touched me deeply.

Human beings have similar thoughts,
feelings and needs, no matter their
country of birth or religion.

Getting Up Close and Personal

Back in Melbourne, as part of our training we rotated to other hospitals. One of my rotations was to the now-defunct Queen Victoria hospital for a term of paediatrics along with general surgical and medical. One of the highlights was being assigned to an intern for an overnight shift, the idea being to receive a little practical experience. We had read and been told about rectal examinations (known to students as a PR for 'per rectum'). Performing one is another matter. Most people know it is used to examine the prostate gland, however, it is an important examination in some acute situations such as helping with the diagnosis of appendicitis or internal bleeding. A full medical examination should include a PR in a male along with a PV (per vagina) in a woman. Consequently, as medical students we did not consider we had learned how to do full examinations until we had performed least one PR and a PV. Strangely, willing patient participants are few and far between. Nevertheless, one gentleman patient in the middle of the night at the Queen Victoria Hospital, allowed me to, under supervision, don a glove apply some lubricant and examine his prostate. Learning to perform a vaginal examination is somewhat different. At least the man was facing away from me and couldn't see how nervous I was. A woman, of course, is looking directly at you and can easily see the sweat on the brow. We were fortunate that the hospital engaged some ladies of the night for us to learn our PV technique. Thankfully, the women were relaxed while we were uptight, and knowing how it should feel, they were able to give us direct feedback in real time. Now, that is a unique experience! Thank you to those women and to that gentleman for helping me gain some confidence in knowing how to fully examine both a male and a female.

It was during fifth-year medicine that I first came into personal contact with Professor Sir ESR Hughes. Sir Edward was the professor of surgery in the Faculty of Medicine at the Alfred Hospital between 1973 and 1984. He was a legend among medical students because of his clear approach to taking a history and performing an examination along with his dry sense of humour. He had what we referred to as 'selective deafness'. You could talk to him and it would appear he was not listening until he responded with an incisive reply just to show he had heard every word. One of the highlights of fifth year was to spend some time with him in his private practice. As a general surgeon, he had a huge colorectal practice, and his patients loved him. In this line of surgery, rectal examinations are more common than taking a patient's blood pressure. For Sir Edward, putting on a glove took too long so he would use a finger stool that fitted over his index finger. This was also expected of every medical student visiting his practice. The problem was, the finger stools didn't quite reach the base of the finger. I recall being very mindful of this as he directed me to perform a PR examination on one of his patients. I quite gingerly inserted my finger up to the length of the stool, at which stage he took my elbow and inserted my finger several more centimetres, with quite obvious consequences. He would always get a chuckle out of this.

Dr Linsell

After the relative relaxation of fifth-year, final-year medicine is quite intense. There is so much to learn, so many patients to see, so many books to read, so many lectures to attend and the available time seems so limited. The final examinations comprise both written and practical components. In the so-called 'long case' we are presented with a patient for us to take a history, examine them and present our findings to a group of clinicians, who then ask us further questions. This is followed by a number of 'short cases' where we are asked to examine a particular area on a patient's body e.g. listen to their heart or examine their abdomen. We again present our findings to a group of clinicians. In answer to one of their questions, I remember making something quite simple into something very complicated.

I agonised about this until the day the results were posted on the wall of the Monash Medical faculty adjacent to the Alfred hospital. I jostled with dozens of other students looking for their name. The names were in order of performance. I wasn't at the top of the list and I held my breath until I saw my name about half way down. Oh my gosh! I had just become a doctor. My friends around me were saying congratulations Doctor and I to them. It was an amazing experience. I felt euphoric, relieved, grateful and so, so excited. I had actually made it. I had passed the medical examination and was soon to be awarded a Bachelor of Medicine and a Bachelor of Surgery (MBBS). What had begun as a small boy's dream, almost 20 years later, was now a reality.

When you know deep within what you
want to do, don't give up.

After applying to various hospitals for my intern year, I was fortunate to receive my first choice, which was the Alfred hospital. The year was divided into four terms. My first appointment was to the Moe Hospital in country Victoria. In retrospect this was a great appointment because I learned very fast on the job. I worked in the operating theatre, the wards and in the emergency department and received an enormous amount of practical experience. In a hospital setting the consultant doctor is usually very experienced and the junior doctors report to them. Some consultants are excellent; others not so much. For instance, on one occasion, I was managing a very sick patient with an acute attack of asthma. It was awful watching this poor man try to take in oxygen with his airway so shut down, he was only getting a small amount into his lungs. I thought he was going to die. Several times, I called my consultant who was at home, giving an update on the patient's condition, pleading with him to come in to the hospital. The consultant kept saying, 'No-one dies from an asthma attack.' I had trouble believing him, watching this man struggling to breathe with the treatment seemingly being ineffective. After what seemed to be an inordinate amount of time, the patient's airway started to open and his breathing became less laboured. He survived, however, it was very scary. Subsequently, I learned that people do die from acute attacks of asthma. In this case, the patient and I were both very fortunate.

When a patient is having a general anaesthetic, it is generally considered appropriate for the anaesthetist to remain with the patient in the operating theatre. There was one infamous anaesthetist who was a smoker. During a long case, his requirement for a cigarette created a problem, as cigarette smoke is not an ideal accompaniment for any surgical procedure. He would therefore put his patient on a ventilator, turn on a microphone in the operating theatre and adjourn to the tearoom for a cigarette, whilst listening by loud speaker to the ventilator. Fortunately, I have never seen anything like this in my subsequent years in surgery.

One consultant who made a mark on me, was a cardiologist named Dr Brett Forge, who had just returned from his specialist training. I enjoyed working for him for he was knowledgeable, enjoyed teaching and was fun. One day he asked me to organise some appointments for a patient of his, in Melbourne. I said I would do so then completely forgot about it. A few weeks later, he contacted me because the patient had arrived in Melbourne and nothing had been arranged. He admonished me and he was absolutely right. In medicine, not following through with a doctor's instructions can have disastrous consequences. From then on, I wrote everything down and each day updated my list of to-dos. This is a practice I continue to this day.

Write stuff down and follow through.

My next appointment was to the emergency department of the Alfred Hospital. At that time, the emergency department was staffed mostly by interns, with a second year doctor allocating beds for admission into the hospital. Thankfully, the people with the most knowledge were the senior nurses who had worked in the department for years. Very early in my career, I learned to listen to the valuable input from experienced nurses. Theoretically, doctors told nurses what to do. However, senior nurses who had been in wards or departments for years, had far more knowledge than young interns. If a young doctor was respectful of the nursing staff, he or she would find the nursing staff only too willing to help out and work as a team. If no respect was shown, the doctor was on his or her own. The nurses in the Alfred emergency department were excellent and together we worked hard to save lives and supported each other when we were unsuccessful.

Death and Life

The emergency department is the sharp end of the brutal edge of life. I had received some of the best training in the world, yet nothing can prepare you for it. For instance, one of my roles was to examine people brought in by ambulance, who were already dead but required a doctor to certify the death. These people didn't even make it into the emergency room so the examination often took place in the dark in the back of an ambulance. Nothing can prepare you for certifying a cot-death baby, still wearing its night-time sleep suit. Or the person, blown up like a pufferfish, who had drowned and had been recently fetched from the Yarra river.

Then there were the burns victims. A full-thickness burn is not painful because all the nerves are destroyed. I recall a man with full thickness burns to 90 per cent of his body. He was not in pain and was fully lucid as his face was one of the few areas not involved. I was chatting with him, yet I knew he would be dead in a few hours and there was nothing I could do. Then there were the people who had a heart attack and their hearts stopped beating. We would pump their chest, intubate them, use the defibrillator, inject drugs and sometimes they would survive. Sometimes they wouldn't. What do you say to a family whose parent or child you have just been working on, has just died? Explaining that a beloved family member has just died is one of the toughest things I have ever had to do. Training had been minimal in this area and for this aspect of medicine, I felt hopelessly underprepared.

Sometimes the emergency department is the last resort for people who have nowhere else to go. One night a teenage girl came in and try as I might to place her, all the usual refuge places were full. She couldn't stay in the department and the next alternative was for her to spend the night on the street. We had a spare bedroom at home, so she slept at my place overnight and I took her back to the hospital the next morning where she went on her way. Was it risky? Possibly. Was it the right thing to do? I think so.

*Sometimes doing the right thing involves
taking a risk.*

My surgical rotation as an intern was to the Monash University Department of Surgery (MUDS) at the Alfred Hospital. I was delighted with this because the head of the unit was Professor Sir Edward Hughes (or ESR as we called him), whom I had met as a fifth-year student. It was a great unit to work in because I worked closely with two young surgical consultants and a surgical registrar who have each gone on to have distinguished careers in surgery. One day, I was part of the surgical team operating on a patient with cancer of the rectum. This involved operating on the abdomen, mobilising the bowel and particularly the rectum, removing the diseased portion, then joining together the two ends of the bowel. The principal surgeon was one of the young consultants just mentioned and ESR was scrubbed (in a sterile surgical gown) but simply observing. The principle surgeon was struggling with a particular manoeuvre that mobilises the rectum. Sweat had formed on his brow and I am sure was trickling down the back of the neck. (I have subsequently had this feeling whilst operating a few times when things aren't going to plan. The feeling is not pleasant.) As the surgeon painstakingly attempted to dissect with scissors and forceps, he didn't seem to be making any progress and it was taking forever. ESR watched patiently for a while, then politely said, 'Let me have a look at this Jim'—'Jim' was not his real name. ESR moved into the primary operating position, assessed the situation and with a few sweeps from side to side with his hand, he mobilised the rectum in seconds. 'Mmm. That should do it,' he said and made way for Jim to complete the rest of the operation. It was beautiful to watch. It was the first time I had observed a surgeon who was truly gifted with his hands. Some just know by feel, when and where to cut, when to stop, when it is safe to use blunt dissection with their hands and how much is required. This is intuitive and whilst most surgeons improve their technique with time and experience, some just get it more quickly.

Some are naturally gifted with a skill that
is Intuitive rather than learned.

Choosing Surgery

I needed to make a decision. It was now the latter half of my intern year. I was clear I wanted to specialise, however, I was considering whether I should follow through with becoming a surgeon or alternatively, become a physician. If I chose surgery, I needed to begin studying in order to sit the first part of the surgical exam the following year. In Australia, there are two parts to the surgical examinations set by the Royal Australasian College of Surgeons (RACS). The first part is sat at the beginning of training. Passing the first part is a prerequisite for commencing training in any of the surgical disciplines. As there are so many applicants for surgical training, the benchmark for passing the first part is deliberately set high in order to select the very best applicants. (I always considered the exam was designed to fail people, however, I know the RACS has a differing view.) Once the first part is passed, the budding surgeon then applies to be trained as a surgical registrar in a particular specialty in a particular hospital. After a minimum of four-years training, the registrar can then sit the second part of the surgical exam. A pass means the registrar then becomes a Fellow of the Royal Australian College of Surgeons (FRACS) giving him or her the right become a surgeon. If the registrar fails, they go back to training and can keep sitting the second part until they pass.

I was discussing the options for my future with the junior consultants when Sir Edward Hughes overheard the conversation. Given his selective deafness, this was unusual in itself. He walked into the room and said, 'You should be a surgeon, Mal!' That was it. That was all I needed. One of the more prominent surgeons in Australia had acknowledged me and knew I had what it takes to be a surgeon. I began studying almost immediately.

There are times in life, where a simple word or action can determine our destiny.

The intern year at a major public hospital is challenging in many ways, not the least of which involves the number of hours worked. It was a normal roster for us to be on call one to two nights per week. On top of that, every four weeks at 7am on a Friday morning, I would don my long white coat, arm myself with my stethoscope and notebook, and know that my shift would not finish until 6pm the following Monday. That is an 83-hour shift where I was constantly on call. When on call, we were required to stay at the hospital in the resident's quarters, where a small room with a bed, a desk and a telephone was provided. We were on call for the emergency department, the wards and any emergencies in the hospital. It was our role to admit new patients (take a history and examine them), order tests, take blood, insert intravenous drips, insert catheters etc. It is a phenomenal commitment of time and energy that seems to be the right of passage for young doctors. I know there were times I was so tired the thought of admitting another elective patient was about as enticing as sticking pins in my eyes, however, I don't recall my clinical judgement being impaired. In an emergency situation, somehow the adrenaline kicks in and concern for the patient overrides everything.

Consequently, studying for a major exam such as the first part is somewhat problematic, when all you want to do when you get home is collapse into bed. I learned to sleep less and get up earlier so I could study before I went to work.

The first part examination in Surgery was held twice a year over two days, consisting of multiple-choice questions in anatomy, pathology and physiology. Candidates can sit the examination as many times as they like, however, each time it costs several thousand dollars. On a young doctor's salary, passing after one sitting is preferable!

Having decided to pursue surgery as a career, my rotations at the Alfred Hospital in second and third year were through different surgical units. Early in my second year I was appointed to the cardiothoracic unit, named after one of Australia's first cardiothoracic surgeons, Sir James Officer Brown. The surgeons in this very busy unit performed multiple heart and lung operations every day. The postoperative care was crucial, monitoring very sick patients, facilitating their recovery after their surgery. By this time, I was a junior resident, which was an appropriate name for I seemed to reside more at the hospital than at home. The job required a 'one-in-two' roster, which meant I slept in the intensive care unit every second night and every second weekend. This worked out to being more than 100 hours a week in the hospital. Thankfully, the nursing staff were exceptional and I learned very quickly to listen and act immediately when experienced nurses recognised danger signs on a patient's monitors.

When I wasn't working, I was studying and practising my cornet. Despite the limited hours of preparation, I sat the first part in mid 1981. We were each given an exam number and when the results were available, we telephoned a secretary at the Royal Australasian College of Surgeons (RACS). She asked for my exam number. I waited with my heart in my mouth. With no emotion, she said, 'I'm sorry, that number has not been successful.'

I was thinking to myself, 'That number is me! I am a person, you know!' I was bitterly disappointed. Some of my colleagues had passed first time and they were either very smart or just seemed to do well with multiple-choice questions. I was neither of those. Nevertheless, giving up was not an option for me. My rotations in the latter half of the year were not quite as demanding and after discussing it with a good friend of mine from the Alfred (who had a similar result to me) we decided to sit again.

When we are on a mission, a temporary
set back is just that. Temporary.

Medical Emergencies

One of my rotations was to the Obstetrics and Gynaecology (O&G) unit. At one stage I had considered specialising in O&G, however, babies tend to be born at all hours of the day and night and getting out of bed in the middle of the night was not something I would look forward to.

Obstetrics patients in a public hospital tend be those who can't afford a private obstetrician or don't want anybody to know they are having a baby. I recall a 19-year-old girl who walked into the emergency department and announced that she was about to have a baby. She had kept it hidden from everybody. I examined her and she was almost fully dilated. We rushed her up to the delivery ward as her labour progressed to full dilation. With most deliveries, the baby presents with the crown of the head first, and once the head is delivered, the baby rotates to deliver the shoulders then the rest of the body, being narrower, comes out easily. In this instance, the baby delivered face first. My obstetric experience was minimal, however, I knew enough to know this was not good. A face presentation changes the angles of the baby's head so that it doesn't move smoothly through the birth canal. I was unable to get hold of a consultant so I was on my own. Once again, thank goodness for the nurses. With their guidance, I made extra room by creating an episiotomy and gently moved the baby's head in order to recreate the normal position for birth. All of this in the middle of a delivery is painful and my young patient was stoic, calm and simply amazing. After what seemed like an eternity, I delivered the baby and placed her on her mother's tummy. What a humbling experience! To facilitate the arrival of another life into the world is one of the truly magical experiences doctors and nurses are privileged to witness.

On another occasion, a lady I had delivered kept bleeding and bleeding, despite drugs given to constrict her uterus. I checked the placenta and noticed parts of it were missing. A baby receives its nourishment in the womb through the umbilical cord. This arises from the placenta, which is attached to the wall of the mother's uterus. Under normal circumstances, when the baby is born, its umbilical cord pulls the placenta away from the uterus and the placenta follows the baby out of the birth canal, leaving a large raw area on the uterus. In order to prevent massive blood loss, the uterus contracts down and this is assisted by drugs administered by the medical staff. If part of the placenta remains attached to the uterus, the uterus cannot contract and the mother continues to bleed. A retained placenta is a medical emergency for if the bleeding is not stopped, the mother can bleed to death. This is what I was faced with. I called the consultant who refused to come in, probably because he knew that if I didn't deal with it, it would be too late. He said, 'You'll be right. Just scrape the placenta off the uterus.'

'What!' I said, not believing what I was hearing. 'What with?'

'Use your hand,' he said.

'You are joking, right?' knowing my patient was exsanguinating in front of my eyes.

'No, I'm not and do it now!' he yelled down the phone.

So again with minimal experience, I inserted my gloved and gowned hand into the birth canal and kept moving my hand up. Soon I was literally up to my elbow in the birth canal and my hand could feel the uterus. I knew if I pressed too firmly, I could rupture the uterus and the lady would die. If I was not firm enough, I wouldn't separate the retained placenta. With my heart in my mouth, I could distinguish the smooth wall of the uterus and could feel what I thought must be the roughened area of placenta. With the side of my hand I moved it back and forth to gently separate the placenta from the uterus. It seemed to come away, first a little bit, then more, until it felt smooth. Cautiously I withdrew my arm, then my hand, followed by a gush of blood and placenta. Quickly we administered more drugs designed to contract the uterus. Had I removed it all? Would the uterus now contract?

Yes. The bleeding stopped. My patient was exhausted but she was alive. It's amazing how the joy of a newborn can override the fact that a few minutes before, she had been perilously close to dying. I have said it before and I say again. Life is very precious.

It was 5.45pm on a Sunday evening and the Camberwell Salvation Army brass band, in full uniform, left the church and turned to march down Athelstan Road in Camberwell. The band marched five abreast. As always the men playing larger instruments were in the front, with the solo cornets in the penultimate row and the percussion behind. We were playing a march, probably a famous one named the 'Red Shield'. It has a solo part at the beginning, which I loved to play. Part way through the march, the tubas and trombones stopped playing, followed by others. Being in the back row we couldn't see what was happening and we kept playing and marching forward. The band was parting, like the Red Sea and as we got to the front of the march, I saw one of my friends, Dave, a tuba player, lying unconscious in the middle of the street. We moved him to the side of the road as I felt for a pulse, not quite believing what was happening. There was no pulse and he wasn't breathing. He had suffered a cardiac arrest. I undid his uniform tunic, remembering the ABC I had been taught. A–Airway, B–Breathing, C–Circulation. I checked his airway, commenced mouth-to-mouth resuscitation, and thumped his chest while someone called an ambulance. I commenced cardiac massage while another friend volunteered to do mouth-to-mouth. The ambulance seemed to take forever, however, we kept working on him, despite there being no response. When the ambulance crew arrived I filled them in while they set up the defibrillator. They shocked him once, then again and for the first time in about 30 minutes, Dave's pulse returned, feebly, but it was palpable. The crew said they would take him to the nearest hospital, however, I asked if they would take him to the Alfred. It was out of their way but they agreed to do so.

Dave was admitted to the Alfred hospital and subsequently to the Cardiothoracic Unit, where I had been working a few months previously. A few days later, after he had been stabilised, Dave underwent coronary artery graft surgery where the arteries that supplied his heart were bypassed using his veins harvested from his leg. I received special permission to view the operation. It was an amazing experience to witness Dave's heart beating freely with new veins attached, when a few days before, it had been lifeless.

Dave made a full recovery and lived quite a few years thereafter. He sent me a Christmas card every year, thanking me for another year that he would otherwise not have had.

Right place; right time. There are times
when another person's destiny is in
our hands.

Choosing Plastic Surgery

Meanwhile, I was still studying for the surgical first part exam. I was still working long hours, however, my study patterns were a little more regular. I resat late in my second year after graduation confident that I had prepared well enough to pass and enter surgical training. I expected the exam to be difficult and the College of Surgeons didn't disappoint me. A couple of weeks later, with some trepidation, I called the RACS hotline and shared my examination number with the same emotionless voice at the other end. 'That number has not been successful.'

I had failed the first part for the second time. I felt as if I had been knocked over by my favourite footballer, Tony Lockett. Feelings of self-doubt poured in as I felt I had tried so hard, yet this was still not good enough. My colleague at the Alfred also failed. He had had enough and refused to be persuaded to sit again. He chose to become a GP, is still practicing and is an excellent doctor. He would have made a great surgeon as well, however, he has no regrets. For me, giving up was not an option. Persistence and resilience are character traits that have served me well over my time. They can also be detrimental, as would become apparent later in my life.

I decided to sit again, in my third year postgraduate year. I felt at the time that I was paying for some gold taps to be installed in the College of Surgeons' bathrooms. Nevertheless, I knew surgery was what I wanted to do. It was during this year that I worked with the plastic surgical unit at the Alfred Hospital and met for the first time, the head of the unit, Mr E John Anstee. John is one of the smartest, funniest men I have ever met. It was he who first put to me the possibility of becoming a plastic surgeon. At that time in Melbourne, the Victorian Plastic Surgical Unit (VPSU) was located at the Preston and Northcote Community Hospital (PANCH). It was founded by the first plastic surgeon in Australia, Sir Benjamin

Rank and was unique in that heads of plastic surgical units and consultants from all around Melbourne operated at the facility, making it a place of surgical excellence. John invited me to come with him to the VPSU and watch him operate. Situated on the fourth floor of PANCH, there were two operating theatres and two wards solely set aside for plastic surgery. On any given day, there might be a repair of a cleft lip and palate in one theatre, with a major reconstruction of a face or leg in another theatre. The amount of the work put through was phenomenal and I was hooked. I decided to become a plastic surgeon.

My reasoning at the time, was four-fold:
1. Plastic surgery was about putting things back (reconstructing) rather than taking things away.
2. It was likely that a cure for cancer would be found in the future and this would have a major impact on many of the surgical specialities. This might not impact plastic surgery quite as much.
3. For many years into the future, people were likely to keep injuring themselves (requiring reconstruction) or want to improve their current appearance.
4. Plastic surgery involved procedures all over the body. I was unlikely to get bored.

The first part exam was scheduled for mid-year of 1982. I had a slight problem. Camberwell Salvation Army Band was scheduled to do a two-week concert tour of the USA, Germany and the UK, with the band returning to Melbourne just a few days prior to the exam. I was the lead cornet player and one of the band's soloists. The tour of the UK would finish with a performance in the Royal Albert Hall, London. It had been a long-held dream of mine to play a solo in the Royal Albert Hall and this was an opportunity that was unlikely to be repeated. One of the great Salvation Army composers, Ray Steadman Allen, had been commissioned to write a piece for our band to play in the Royal Albert Hall. Entitled 'At the Edge of Time', it was a piece that challenged the band yet when played well, was inspiring to listen to. In spite of my long working hours, I had been practicing my cornet for one to two hours a day for 12 months in preparation for the trip. (When I couldn't practise at home, I would practise in the soundproof audiology room at the hospital. My beeper still worked whilst I was in the room and I could play as loud as I wanted because no-one could hear me.) Under normal circumstances, I would take two weeks leave prior to the exam and study all day. Going on an overseas trip, performing on most nights and travelling through the day, meant study would be next to impossible.

I discussed the dilemma with my surgical supervisors. One of them said, 'If you go on that trip, you are an idiot!' That was comforting! I thought about it; prayed about it. Somehow, in my heart, I just knew it would be okay. I decided to go on the trip—carrying a thick pathology textbook in my carry-on luggage.

The Royal Albert Hall—Finally!

Salvation Army Brass Band tours are generally a lot of fun. Forty men with similar values, aiming to be and play the best they can, in front of enthusiastic, often sell out crowds, with the purpose of entertaining and inspiring in a spiritual sense. As the men are often billeted with different families in different cities each night, lifelong friendships are often developed. This trip was phenomenal.

When we arrived in the UK, Britain and Scotland were undergoing a heatwave. Having played, on occasions, in 40-degree heat in Australia, this was not unusual for us, however, at one of our concerts in Scotland, 30-degree weather was extremely unusual, so much so, that they were unable to turn off the heaters in the concert hall. To play a brass instrument requires a reasonable embouchure, however, this was somewhat difficult to maintain with sweat pouring down our faces.

The tour was nearing completion and I knew our bandmaster was wrestling with a dilemma. Our band was due to play two pieces in the Royal Albert Hall. One was the piece commissioned for that specific occasion. The other was to be a solo piece played by one of our soloists. The bandmaster had three main soloists to choose from. One was Russell Davies, a brilliant euphonium soloist, who also happened to be the bandmaster's son. The others were Jeff McLaren an outstanding trombone soloist and myself. Russell was younger, more talented and seemed to do things so much easier than I did, with much less practise. I, on the other hand, needed to practise and practise, yet still was not quite as good.

It was therefore not surprising to me, that Brian took me aside a few days before the end of the tour to tell me that he had decided Russell would be playing at the Royal Albert Hall. Although I would have loved to play a solo at the Royal Albert Hall, Russell fully deserved the opportunity and it was the right decision.

To play at the Royal Albert Hall is an experience never to be forgotten. To be on the stage and look out into an audience of around 5000, packed into the circular stadium is awe-inspiring. The Salvation Army knows how to put on a concert and this was no exception. Russell played his solo, accompanied by the band, and he was brilliant. We played our set piece (which included some solo parts for cornet) and we were very good—as good as we had ever played. It had been a dream of mine to play a solo in the Royal Albert Hall. I didn't quite achieve the goal, however, I had the privilege of sharing an experience with my mates in one of the most esteemed venues in world music.

After that exhilarating experience, it was time to return home to sit an exam that would determine my future career. I had studied on the first stopover and after that had given the study away. I returned tired, yet personally inspired by the experience and the wonderful people I had met.

Sweeter the Third Time

I sat the exam a few days later. I am not sure that I knew more. It was as though I had an inner confidence. That confidence, however, evaporated when…well, you know the drill by now! I called that fateful number and spoke to the same woman at the College of Surgeons. I recited my number…

'You have been successful. Congratulations.' She was different; she was warm. 'Really', I said. 'Are you sure?'

'Yes', she said. 'You have passed. Congratulations.'

Oh my gosh. I had done it.

I was going to become a surgeon.

Dad was at work. I went to see Mum. I walked in and she looked at me with expectation in her face. 'Mum. I did it.' I said. We hugged and cried together. I think it meant a lot to Mum, particularly as she had been looking after me when I had burned my hand as a child. She didn't say it but I knew she was very proud of me.

Achievement of a dream can mean just as much to those who have supported you as it does to you.

Australia has some of the most stringent requirements in the world for becoming a surgeon. In Australia, once a doctor has passed the first part, at least another four years of approved training is required before the second part of the surgical exam can be attempted. The requirements and exams are set in place by the Royal Australian College of Surgeons. When the doctor has passed the second part, he or she becomes a Fellow of the Royal Australian College of Surgeons (FRACS). The FRACS is hard to achieve and only those who have these letters after their name have been fully trained and qualified as surgeons in Australia.

This is confusing to the general public. When I graduated as a doctor I gained a Bachelor of Medicine and a Bachelor of Surgery. (MBBS) The Bachelor of Surgery part of my qualifications theoretically means I can legally perform surgery. However, there is a major difference between knowing a small part of the theory of some surgical techniques and actually doing them. It is unfortunate, to say the least, that some doctors with an MBBS after their name (and no FRACS), advertise and perform surgery on an unsuspecting public.

Learning How To Cut

To enter the plastic surgical training program, it was prudent to have completed a year of general surgical training. I applied for and was accepted for a 12-month position as a surgical registrar at the Alfred Hospital. I found I couldn't learn to do surgery just by reading a book. I learn best by watching someone else do the procedure first, then duplicating his or her movements. The better the teacher is with their hands and the better I am with mimicking their movements, the more quickly I learn. The opposite is also true. If the teacher lacks dexterity, it is best not to replicate their mistakes. The best surgeons are confident and realistic in their ability. Some are overconfident and they are to be avoided. It might sound strange but good surgeons know how to cut. For instance, they will make one cut in the skin or elsewhere, with the right pressure and the right depth and then move to the next layer. Others make multiple movements, like scratching, in order to make the same incision. This takes extra time for the same result. If you multiply this extra time by countless incisions made during an operation, you start to get some idea why some procedures take longer in some surgeon's hands. Thankfully, a surgeon's efficiency (and reduced complication) rate generally improves with time. Generally speaking, experienced surgeons who are efficient with their movements and technique have reduced complication rates and *all* surgeons have complications. If a surgeon tells you they have no complications, they are either not being honest or not doing enough surgery. In either case, run!

During my first six months of surgical training, I was shown how to diagnose and perform reasonably simple operations such as an appendectomy. After a while I was able to do these without supervision. However, whilst performing a cholecystectomy— looking down a deep dark hole trying to differentiate the common bile duct from the cystic artery—I had a suspicion this was not the type of surgery I wanted to be doing on a long-term basis.

Vascular surgery is the surgical treatment of blood vessels damaged by disease or trauma. Arteries carry blood and nutrients to organs and limbs so they can function effectively. When the arteries are diseased or blocked, the blood flow decreases and the areas previously supplied cease to function or die due to the lack of blood supply. Diseased blood vessels are often the end result of smoking. It never ceased to amaze me that people would rather have their toes or legs amputated than give up smoking.

Because minor surgical errors in this type of surgery, can have catastrophic results, it requires a surgeon to have manual dexterity as well as a temperament that allows them to perform well under pressure. I was appointed the Vascular Surgery registrar, which was unusual as a more experienced trainee usually filled this position. Nevertheless, the opportunity to work with a team of high quality surgeons, with both elective and emergency cases, was an exceptional opportunity. One of the surgeons was particularly gifted in performing an elective carotid endarterectomy. This is required when there is a build up of plaque on the wall of the carotid artery, the main blood vessel supplying the brain. The plaque can either flick off little pieces of debris or completely occlude the artery, both of which will lead to a stroke and even death. The operation involves an incision on one side of the neck, identifying, then clamping the artery. This is delicate, as this manoeuvre itself, can cause a stroke. The artery is then opened, the plaque gently separated from the wall of the artery and then removed. The artery is then sutured and the clamp removed. If the suture repair of the artery is incomplete, blood will burst through the wall and this again can put the patient at risk. Fortunately, the surgeon I worked with was one of those who just knew intuitively what to do. His work was exceptional and I learned an enormous amount just by watching and assisting him.

An abdominal aortic aneurysm (AAA) is a weakness in the wall of the main blood vessel that carries blood directly from the heart. The wall gets thin and might balloon out, requiring an operation to replace the diseased segment of the aorta. If this is an elective procedure, it usually proceeds quite routinely. If, however, the aneurysm bursts this is a medical emergency as the patient can quickly bleed to death. Even if the patient can get to hospital and into the operating theatre, only 50 per cent survive. Time is of the essence. The faster the patient can get to the operating theatre, the more chance they have of staying alive.

During my time as the Vascular Registrar, a ruptured AAA seemed most likely to occur in the early hours of the morning. As I was on call for the unit 24-hours of the day, it was my role to be present for all of them. Late one Sunday evening I was called to the emergency department for a suspected ruptured AAA. The patient had experienced severe abdominal pain and collapsed at home, was rushed to hospital and resuscitated by the team in the emergency department. When I examined his abdomen, he had a palpable lump that throbbed in time with his heartbeat, which is the telltale sign of an AAA. He required an immediate operation to repair the damaged artery and save his life. I called the surgeon, booked the operating theatre and made sure there was blood on standby. By this stage it was early on Monday morning.

Patients with a ruptured AAA have already lost a lot of blood out of the aorta, however, this is contained in their abdomen. It is only when the abdominal cavity is entered, during the surgery, that the blood is released. This is a critical time of the operation, because the patient's blood pressure can drop precipitously. A great anaesthetist, working in team with the surgeon, can make such a difference at this critical time.

In this instance all went well. A long incision was made in the midline of the abdomen to give access to the aorta, which lies at the back of the abdominal cavity. We were able to clamp the aorta, replace the diseased segment of aorta with a synthetic blood vessel, unclamp the aorta, making sure the join didn't leak, then close the patient's abdomen in layers. The patient went to the Intensive Care Unit (ICU) postoperatively and subsequently made a full recovery. The whole process took about five hours, so as I was putting on my white coat to leave the operating theatre, surgeons were arriving to do their normal Monday morning operating lists. I attempted to shave using a hospital razor and found it more dangerous than the scalpel we had been using overnight. I went straight to the Monday morning ward round looking like a cross between Barry Gibb and Norman Gunston.

It had been a tough day, when, later that evening, I finally made it home to fall into bed. Just as I was preparing, the phone rang. It was the emergency department at the Alfred. They were sorry to disturb me (they usually are) but they had just received a patient with a likely ruptured AAA. I said goodbye to my bed and drove into the hospital. This patient was in a worse condition than the previous night's. He was severely ill and the chances of him surviving an operation were not high, however, he had no chance if we didn't operate. By the time he got to theatre, it was again the early hours of the morning. A different consultant surgeon was called in to perform the operation. We worked hard, however, his vessels were crumbly and we had trouble getting sutures to hold without leaking. The operation took about four hours and when we came to suture his abdomen, he was so swollen we couldn't get the edges together. The surgeon explained to me that in his experience, it would be unlikely that the patient would survive the next 24 hours. This is invariably a difficult situation for the surgical team, who work tirelessly to provide the best possible care for patients. When you know, in spite of your best efforts, that a patient is not going to make it, it is terribly sad. The surgeon's prediction was correct and the patient passed away in ICU within a few hours.

Surgical Orgasm?

Daylight was again filtering into the hospital corridors, when I left the operating theatre for the ward round on Tuesday morning. This time I went unshaven, (not a good look), however, most senior surgeons and nursing staff, know that occasionally young doctors might not be looking their best. I hadn't slept for two nights and, fortunately, later that afternoon, I was able to catch a couple of hours' nap before I headed off to band practice. This was a welcome break from the pressure environment of the hospital and I was enjoying playing even when we were not living up to the bandmaster's high expectations. Part way through the rehearsal, my beeper buzzed. I couldn't believe it. My immediate thought was to stuff it down one of the tubas and ignore it, however, this was not a long-term solution.

I called the number displayed on the beeper and it was answered by one of the consultant surgeons.

SR: 'Mal, we have a ruptured abdominal aneurysm and we need to operate now. When can you get here?'

ML: 'Sammy, you have got to be joking. This is my third night in a row. I don't think I can do it!'

SR: 'Of course you can son. You are about to have a surgical orgasm!'

Well what could I say to that? Being a fine, upstanding Salvation Army lad, this sounded good to me.

I headed into the hospital and assisted him with the third ruptured AAA in three nights. Whilst he was a very experienced surgeon, he was not afraid of blood and was often covered in it at the end of an operation. If during an operation, he ever said, 'Whoops', I had learned to duck, because it usually meant a vessel had been nicked and blood would spurt everywhere.

Nevertheless, on this occasion, he was at his best and everything went smoothly. He repaired the aneurysm in good time and the patient went off to ICU as usual. A few days later he was discharged to the ward and eventually went home.

I was able to get home for a few hours sleep before the ward round on Wednesday morning, when I was showered, shaved and dressed appropriately. However, talk about delayed gratification, I am still waiting for that surgical orgasm to this day!

It was experiences such as those mentioned, where I was stretched to the limit physically and mentally, that helped to mould my character. Dealing with emergency situations—where one false move can result in a critical outcome—is sobering yet extraordinarily fulfilling. I have learned not to panic, to remain calm, remember medical and surgical principles and take the necessary action. The patient and their families feel the confidence that comes with this. Patients want to trust their doctor. When they know that no matter what, they will not be abandoned and the doctor will always act in their best interests, they will willingly allow the doctor to care for them. As a younger doctor, I didn't fully understand this and often took this trust for granted. Nowadays, I never do and it is one of the most humbling and rewarding facets of medical practice.

Character is moulded by
overcoming physical, mental and
emotional challenges.

Now that I had some experience with general surgery, vascular surgery, obstetrics and gynaecology, it was clear to me that I really wanted to be a plastic surgeon. That entailed applying for and being accepted into the plastic surgical training program. Applications were made to the appropriate authorities and it was commonplace for the candidates to seek interviews with the heads of the plastic surgical units of the major public hospitals around Melbourne. These were informal interviews, where I was asked why I wanted to be a plastic surgeon and my training to date. Compared with the interview process nowadays, they were quite relaxed, however, the quality of the candidates was outstanding and there were only four positions available.

Late in 1983, I received a call from the head of the plastic surgical unit of the Royal Children's Hospital in Melbourne. I listened to what he had to say and was sure he might be able to hear my heart beating through my chest. He told me that I had been accepted into the plastic surgical training program and I was to commence work at the Victorian Plastic Surgical Unit (VPSU) at the Preston and Northcote Community Hospital (PANCH) in February 1984.

I was going to become a plastic surgeon!

Part Four
Plastic Surgery and Wesley

The Victorian Plastic Surgical Unit

The Victorian Plastic Surgical Unit (VPSU) was unique in that it was a centre of excellence for plastic surgery attracting the very best plastic surgeons from around Melbourne. It was a rich learning environment with constant stimulation from world-class surgeons, each of whom had their own specialties. Some were reconstructive, specialising in complex reconstructions of the face, breast or limbs, where a large block of tissue might be harvested from one part of the body (complete with its blood vessels), transferred to another part of the body and with the blood vessels reconnected under a microscope. The planning, dexterity and patience required for such surgery was immense, with procedures often taking 12 hours or more and involving different teams of surgeons. After the surgery, the plastic surgical registrar was required to stay in the hospital to monitor the patient overnight. Thankfully this was not quite as onerous as some of my previous on call work.

If a large defect is created either through cancer excision or trauma, the best means of reconstructing the defect is using similar tissue. For instance, if the defect is missing bone and muscle and skin, it is best reconstructed with a block of tissue (or flap) comprising bone and muscle and skin. In this way large defects of the face and jaw can be reconstructed using a flap of bone, muscle and skin from the hip or leg, however, for a piece of tissue this large and complex to stay alive, it requires its own blood supply. One of the surgeons at the VPSU, Mr Ian Taylor, had spent hours of research identifying the blood supply to various flaps around the body, so he could use these in his world-pioneering work. These flaps required at least one artery to bring blood to the flap and sometimes more importantly, a vein to take blood away. When a flap (including its blood vessels) is removed from one part of the body, to keep it alive, the blood vessels need to be reattached, under the microscope, to blood vessels near the defect. This is the crucial part of this type of free flap surgery. If the artery occludes, the flap dies because no blood is flowing into it and the tissue fails to receive nutrients. If the vein blocks off, the flap also dies because blood cannot flow through the tissue as the outlet is blocked.

Monitoring the blood supply to the flap was the role of the plastic surgical registrar. This meant that on an hourly basis, the flap would be prodded to assess its viability. Skin and underlying tissue (in a white-skinned person) is usually pink. When prodded, it blanches, then, when the pressure is removed, the pink returns. If the artery is blocked, the skin is initially white, feels cold, and, when prodded, the indentation remains. If the vein is blocked, the skin is purple, swollen and doesn't blanch. Both scenarios usually mean a return to the operating theatre so the blood supply can be re-established.

Sometimes the flap can be going well for a few days then a blockage occurs. In this scenario, it is usually the vein that blocks off first. A return to theatre at this stage might compromise the artery, which is functioning perfectly well. A temporary solution is required. What if there was something that will take blood away from tissue for a few days? This would give time for new veins to grow into the tissue and take the blood away naturally. Well, Mother Nature provided us with an effective solution. It is called a leech.

Believe it or not, leeches are grown just for this purpose. One or more leeches are placed on the flap with an occluded vein and as the leech starts sucking blood away, the area surrounding it starts to pink up. When the leech has had enough, it falls off and another one is applied. I recall a patient who required a complex reconstruction of his face, jaw and neck following removal of a large cancer. In order to reconstruct the defect effectively, he required a tracheostomy. When his flap started to deteriorate a few days later, leeches were applied to the reconstructed area on his face and neck. I was always a bit concerned that an enterprising leech would wander down his tracheostomy tube. Fortunately, this didn't occur and after a few days of leech treatment, the flap was rescued and all was well. The leeches were also happy.

Another unique aspect of the VPSU was the standard of nursing care. The unit, staffed by some of the best nurses I have ever had the privilege of working with, ran a postgraduate course in plastic surgical nursing care. Jill Storch, the unit manager, was exceptional. She was committed to excellence and reputation or title meant little to her. If a surgeon, or more particularly, a registrar, was not living up to the standards of the unit, she made it very clear this was unacceptable. When Jill would scrub with me, every stitch had to be perfect, otherwise she would slap me on the hand, tell me to take it out and do it again. (I think she reminded me of my mother!) It is amazing how humiliation is a great motivator to excellence. Because of her experience, she could tell very quickly, whether a registrar had the capacity to be a consultant surgeon. She intuitively knew which registrar had a good pair of hands and if not, if they were open to being taught. Similarly, she knew which registrars were not suited to plastic surgery and her observations were taken into account when our superiors were determining our future careers.

It was at the VPSU that I first came into contact with Mr Murray James Stapleton, plastic surgeon and Dr Joseph Marich, anaesthetist. Joe had worked with Murray for some time and together they were simply the best combination of surgeon and anaesthetist I have ever had the good fortune to work with. Both men were exceptionally intelligent and gifted in their fields. Murray had the fastest pair of hands I have witnessed. Every movement was specific and effective, developed and honed by him, to give the best result in the most efficient manner. Murray taught me how to use my hands in the most effective and efficient manner possible and much of my current surgical skill I owe to his patience, willingness to teach and openness to sharing his insights. Murray became my mentor and it is from him that I first began to learn about the nuances of cosmetic surgery, what patients were looking for and how to give them what they wanted.

Together, Joe and Murray were two of the funniest individuals I know and they made it fun to work with them. I learned that when the surgical team (surgeon, anaesthetist, nursing staff and theatre technicians) are enjoying themselves, the theatre flows. Patients pick up on this and enjoy the experience so much more.

Fun in the Workplace

There is no question that the VPSU was the most fun place to work during my training. For instance, it was the only place where I needed to be conscious of my underwear before I left for work everyday, because it was highly likely that my jocks would be exposed at any time during the day. Before you jump to a less than complimentary conclusion, let me explain. To work in the operating theatre, we would normally wear white overalls and when scrubbed for an operation, we would put on a sterile gown and gloves as an outer layer. Sterility is important during an operation to prevent infection. This is why the patient is prepped with antiseptic and covered with sterile drapes. As long as the operating team stays adjacent to the sterile operating field, sterility is maintained and the chance of infection is greatly reduced. The sterile gown worn by a surgeon needs to be tied up from behind by a member of the team who is unsterile.

During some of the longer cases, as mentioned above, there are times where both the surgical assistants (sterile) and the observing staff (unsterile) might just be a little bored. On more than one occasion, whilst I was maintaining my sterility by facing the sterile field, a member of the nursing staff would access the back of my gown and with scissors begin cutting away the bottom half of my overalls. I, of course, could do nothing to prevent this, for any movement on my behalf was likely to irritate the operating surgeon or compromise sterility. Consequently, it was not unknown for the lower part of my overalls to hit the floor, exposing my underwear to all who walked behind me. I would complete the procedure with the air conditioning gently swirling around my nether regions and when the patient's dressing was in place, subtly retrieve my trousers from the floor and head for the change room!

On another occasion, I was assisting a quite serious plastic surgeon. This entailed standing on the opposite side of the table from him, placing my hands or retractors to enable him to see the operation more clearly as well as stopping any bleeding. To stop bleeding required using forceps to pick up the vessel then use my foot to stand on the diathermy pedal, completing an electrical circuit through the patient, which cauterised the blood vessel. The operation was well underway when I felt some movement around my ankles. A member of the nursing staff thought it might be rather funny to plaster my feet together. Plaster starts as long rolls, which, when wet, can be wrapped around objects quite easily. It sets rock hard within a few minutes. As I was unable to move, the offending nurse was able to wrap my ankles in a figure of eight fashion that was highly effective in converting my feet into a single unit. This wouldn't have been so much of an issue if I didn't have to use my feet, however, every time I needed to use the diathermy pedal, I would waddle from side-to-side like a penguin. To his credit the surgeon either didn't seem to notice or ignored the strange behaviour of his assistant.

When the case was finished, I waited for the surgeon to leave the theatre then kangaroo hopped my way to where the plaster shears were kept. This of course was accompanied by raucous laughter from all others in the operating suite. Outside each theatre, were taps over a long, deep sink where we would wash our hands before each procedure. I plugged the outlet, filled the sink with cold water, added some Betadine and after a short chase, ever so gently, placed the offending nurse in the sink.

*A fun workplace doesn't have to
compromise standards or effectiveness.*

Murray also gave me an insight into the importance of life balance. He would relate a story to me of when he had flown one his mentors, a doyen in plastic surgery who now had a terminal illness, across the country to Broome, Western Australia. As the two men stood on the beach, looked out over the Indian Ocean and watched the sun set, the mentor said that this was the most beautiful site he had ever seen. Murray would comment that whilst Broome is indeed beautiful, there are so many other stunning sites in the world, that his mentor would never have the privilege of visiting. His mentor had devoted his life to his career and whilst enormously respected by his patients and peers alike, had burned himself out and was dying too young.

The VPSU was a great opportunity to not only observe and learn the technical side of plastic surgery but also to observe the plastic surgeons themselves. It became clear to me that spending hours and hours reconstructing complex cases and observing them on an hourly basis was not for me. I could see that this would be rewarding, however, the time required would come at a cost of life balance. Thank goodness, there are many surgeons that knowingly dedicate themselves to such a career and we are all the richer for it. On the other hand, Murray's personality and approach were different. He had a huge practice because he gave his patients great value, he was a great surgeon, and because his patients knew he cared for them. This was the sort of plastic surgery and the type of practice I wanted to have.

Towards the middle of my second year at the VPSU, I started to become restless and bored. Here I was, being trained for the career of my dreams, in one of the world's best facilities, with access to world class surgeons and I was beginning to have second thoughts. As I look back, I can see this has happened a few times in my life, particularly when things are going well. It is a form of self-sabotage. At one stage I was even considering leaving medicine and entering full-time ministry.

I had what I thought was a bright idea. I thought it would be good to get out of the unit for a period of time so I arranged with a head of unit to visit his hospital once a week to attend the plastic surgical ward round and outpatient clinic. Unfortunately, this would clash with my weekly operating session with Murray, however, I assumed he would see how brilliant my idea was. Big mistake. Murray was furious and let me know in no uncertain terms.

This was a communication issue. My communication with Murray was poor and in particular, I did not seek his input before I made the decision.

Effective communication is one of the
greatest skills to learn.

Plastic Surgery for Rats

One of the options available to surgical trainees was the opportunity to do a year of research, which would count as an accredited year of training. An opportunity arose for me to do some research in plastic surgery at Prince Henry's Hospital in Melbourne. This was one of the best decisions I had made to date, for it gave me some time away from the pressure of clinical work whilst still stretching my thought processes. In 1996, I commenced my research year and after some discussion with my superiors, we decided on a project that would explore the possibility of storing free flaps for later use. As mentioned previously, a free flap is a block of tissue detached from its blood supply in one area of the body, then transplanted to another area and reconnected with a new blood supply. The transfer to another part of the body is usually done immediately, however, there might be times when this is not appropriate and storing the tissue for a period of time might be beneficial. Previous research workers at Prince Henry's Hospital had developed a model for kidney transplantation in rats, using various storage solutions, which then went on to be used in human patients. The laboratories and expertise at Prince Henry's were second to none.

Free flaps often combine bone, muscle and skin in a block of tissue. I developed a free flap model in a rat that harvested a block of bone, muscle and skin from one rat and transplanted it into another otherwise identical rat. The trick was learning to reconnect the blood vessels under a microscope. Rat blood vessels are of course considerably smaller than most human vessels so it took me several months to perfect the technique and have a working model that could be replicated. The skill I learned was invaluable. Apart from free flap surgery, a plastic surgeon often works under a microscope to repair damaged blood vessels and nerves following trauma to hands and fingers. Near the tip of the finger, the vessel size is about the same as the rat vessels I was repairing.

Towards the end of the year, it became clear that I would require more than 12 months to complete the research. The options were for me to continue the research part-time or take another year and submit the work for a Masters of Surgery or even do further work and receive a PhD. Although I quite liked the idea of being a 'Doctor Doctor', this would probably take three years. A further year resulting in a Masters of Surgery (MS), which was quite rare for plastic surgeons in those days, sounded good. This second year would not count towards my surgical training, however, even if I didn't win a Nobel Prize, I felt an MS would always be a bonus. 1997 was therefore also committed to research.

As I could more or less choose the hours for my research, these two years also gave me an opportunity to do some other things. Firstly, in order to get some more experience (and some funds) I was able to be a surgical assistant for my plastic surgical mentors, Mr Stapleton, Mr Anstee and Mr Donald Marshall. Each of these gentlemen were gifted surgeons and to stand on the other side of the operating table to them, listening, watching and learning was an exceptional experience. Learning the technical aspects of surgery, I suspect, is similar to being an apprentice whilst learning a trade. Good apprentices learn to mimic the movements of their bosses. Young surgeons are no different. Masters of surgical technique have developed their skill over time in order to be efficient and above all safe. Seemingly a small incision here or a stitch there can make a major difference to the outcome of any surgical procedure. Mimicking a master is the fastest and safest way to learn.

I spent two years, assisting three of Melbourne's best surgeons, learning to put my hands in the right place, learning to suture, learning how to get out of difficult situations, learning how to manage my time, learning how to communicate with patients in the private sector who were often having cosmetic surgery. The experience was invaluable and helped to set me up for my future career.

Leaning to mimic a master is the fastest
and safest way to learn.

The Cost of Discipleship Tour

The second thing I had more time for was practising my cornet. Brian Davies was still the bandmaster of Camberwell Salvation Army band and I was still the lead cornet player. Brian had arranged for the band to do another international tour, this time to Singapore, Scandinavia and the UK. Along with the extra band rehearsals, I committed to practicing at least two hours a day so I could be in the best form possible when we toured. To do this, I would be up at 5am, exercise, then practise for an hour before going to the hospital to work on the rats, or assisting, or both. At the end of the day I would practise for another hour before falling into bed. For me to play well, I had to practise every day. If I missed one day, I would notice. If I missed two days, other people would notice. As a band we practised and practised and alone I practised and practised as well. When a group of 40 people commit to excellence, with all willing to do their very best, there is a special bond that develops between them. In a Salvation Army band there is something extra as well. Each person sees this as part of their spiritual expression, believes they have a God-given talent, and want to give of their best to inspire others. It is very unique and very fulfilling to be part of such a group.

Brian was an excellent bandmaster. He would teach, train, cajole and sometimes beg us to play better, mostly while retaining his creative sense of humour. To motivate a group of 40 volunteers to find extra time in their workdays and weekends to practise is no mean feat. Yet Brian always seemed to bring out the best in a group of men. He had the same effect on me. His personal success as a cornet player and as a pharmacist, as well as his ability to lead a group of men was always an inspiration to me. He consistently demonstrated that there was always another way. If he set his mind to achieve something, he seemed to overcome all obstacles. He was a mentor to me for more than 20 years and I am richer for the time and attention he gave me.

As a soloist, I was expected to have two to three solos prepared for the tour and any one of these could be chosen for any particular night. My main solo was entitled 'Song of Exultation'. I had first heard it played by Richard Martin, a cornet soloist in London, a couple of years previously and it thrilled me. I purchased the recording and listened to his interpretation over and over. As in surgery, I tried to mimic his playing. My talent was not in the same league as Richard's, however, in listening and playing in a similar fashion, I got to the stage where I loved playing it. It was a challenging solo, but when played well, thrilled the audience. When I played there were times when I felt I was channelling something or someone deeply spiritual. It was an amazing feeling and can only come about when I have put in the work, know that I am doing my best and simply relax, knowing that the notes will flow. When I was in that zone, people would tell me they had been uplifted and moved. This made all of the long hours of practice very worthwhile.

When the band flew out of Australia, we were playing better than ever before. The tour of Norway, Sweden and Denmark was magnificent. We seemed to be treated like royalty in each place we visited. With tongue in cheek, some of the guys named it the 'Cost of Discipleship' tour. I think Dietrich Bonhoeffer might have turned in his grave. Nevertheless, the band played well and we had a lot of fun. The Scandinavians are not an unattractive lot so it was quite entertaining to march down the main streets of Copenhagen and Stockholm and be surrounded by beautiful women along the way. I was, of course, only doing some research for my future career!

On one occasion at one of our venues in England, we were dressed in our uniforms, preparing to file onto stage for the evening concert. There was a frantic knock on the door and a member of the audience asked if there was a doctor in the band. I introduced myself and learned that someone had collapsed in the audience. I rushed into the concert hall to discover someone was lying straddled over the seats, halfway up a stepped auditorium. I raced up the stairs and saw the man was pale, unresponsive, not breathing and had no pulse. It was impossible to work on him in between the seats, so members of his family helped me carry him down the steps to the front of the stage. Meanwhile they told me he had a heart condition and had not been well recently. He had clearly had a cardiac arrest so I began to perform cardiac massage at the front of the stage in front of about 500 people. Meanwhile, the rest of the band, unaware of what was going on, filed onto the stage to take up their positions for the concert. There was a deathly silence in the auditorium as I worked on the gentleman until the ambulance arrived. This was rural England and unfortunately they did not have a defibrillator available. They transported him to the waiting ambulance while I kept working on him, however, after about 45 minutes of no response and with agreement from the ambulance staff, I reluctantly stopped. This is one of the most heart-wrenching decisions a doctor has to make. Whilst you are still pumping somebody's chest there is still hope. As soon as you stop, the person is declared deceased. It is likely this gentleman had died as soon as he collapsed, however, it is still a very empty feeling to know I had tried and failed to revive him. I explained what had happened to the family members who were gathered close by and did what I could to console them. It seemed that his passing was not totally unexpected and they were grateful for what I had been able to do.

The concert was well under way when I rejoined the band. It was a weird experience trying to refocus on the music and play my best. Thank goodness for my fellow cornet players who took over the lead when they sensed I was lagging a little. This is the value of team, which, in my arrogance, I didn't fully appreciate at that time in my life, however, I couldn't have done what I have done, without the support of countless others in so many ways.

I wasn't due to play a solo that night, yet during the interval, I received a message that the family of the deceased man had requested I play 'The Old Rugged Cross' as a solo in the second half. It was one of the most moving things I have ever done. I felt honoured and very blessed.

Some of life's richest moments flow out
of tragedy.

We had had a fabulous tour and our final concert was to be held at the Portsmouth Guildhall. A few nights previously, Brian told me he wanted me to play a solo at this event. On the night of the performance, although I was a little nervous, I was strangely calm. On most occasions before I played, my mouth would be dry (which is less than ideal for playing a brass instrument) and my palms sweaty. On this night I had a quiet confidence. I had practised long and hard, so I was well prepared to do my best. From a young age, I had learned to play without music. Forgetting the notes was, of course, a disaster, however, I quickly learned that if I thought too much about the next note, I was likely to make a mistake. If I relaxed and let it go, the notes would flow.

It was a combined concert with other bands and when we took our places on the stage, there were about 2000 people in the audience. After the first few items, it was time. I was to play 'Song of Exultation', which had become my favourite solo. Brian introduced me and I stood to the warm applause of the audience.

It doesn't matter how good a soloist is, if the accompaniment is lacklustre the soloist has to work harder. Similarly, if the soloist is having an off night, the band has to work harder. The centre of a stage can be a lonely place on nights such as that. On a few such occasions, if I wasn't doing so well, I am sure Brian was singing louder than I was playing! Nevertheless, on this night, from the moment the accompaniment started, I could feel the band wanting me to do well. They were on. Then, when I started playing, the notes seemed to flow. I was on as well. The solo has three movements, two fast and a slow middle movement. The middle movement is based on two hymn tunes and as I was playing I would sing them in my head. 'My Jesus I love thee' and then the more dramatic, 'And He rose again and He lives in my heart, where all is peace and perfect love.' I played what I believed. It was meaningful for me and I wanted to connect with and communicate with the audience.

The final movement just flew and as I finished on a high 'D', the audience was already applauding. There is nothing quite so thrilling and humbling, when you know you have given everything you have and the audience is very appreciative. Rather than bow, I gave the Salvation Army salute, with my index finger pointing to the heavens, acknowledging the Source of any talent. It was the best I had ever played and it was very satisfying.

Sometimes, all the hard work and sacrifice culminate in an experience that makes it all worthwhile.

Moving in Mysterious Ways

After returning to Melbourne, I spent time finishing off my research project, then began the long process of collating the data and putting it into a form that was acceptable as a thesis. I was anxious to be back into clinical work rather than spend a further year with the possibility of a PhD. However, I was still a little restless and I was contemplating whether there might be options other than completing my training in Melbourne. Out of the blue, I received one of those phone calls that changed my life forever. One of my mentors, Mr John Anstee, head of plastic surgery at the Alfred Hospital, called to say he had become aware of a plastic surgical registrar position that was vacant for the following year at St Thomas' Hospital in London. The opportunity to work in London was extraordinary. Most trainees at the time completed their training in Australia then went overseas for further experience. Always willing to consider opportunities outside the box, I had to weigh up the risk of going outside the norm, compared with the experience of living and working in one of my favourite countries. I wrestled with the decision, thinking and praying about it. One morning I was reading the Bible and this verse seemed to jump out of the page at me. 'The LORD had said to Abram, go from your country, your people and your father's household to the land I will show you.' (Genesis 12:1 New International Version)

That was it. I was going and I had no further hesitation. I called John to accept the position and began to set plans in place to live overseas for a couple of years. I think my ability to move location with little notice stems from my childhood experiences of moving states, houses and schools every few years. I had just turned 33, was single and heading overseas.

During my time at university and subsequent hospital-based training, my priorities had been medicine and the cornet. I had not been ready to settle down because I didn't make time available for long-term relationships. Not that I had taken any monastic vows. I had quite a few, shall we say, brief relationships over that time and thankfully I am still on speaking terms with many of those ladies through Facebook.

Nevertheless, it was felt by many that I was unlikely to return to Australia unmarried, so it was decided that my wedding breakfast should be celebrated before I left. There was just one small problem; I did not have bride. My anaesthetist, Joseph Maria Marich came to the rescue and very kindly, volunteered to become my betrothed for the occasion. Wedding invitations were prepared and requested that people come dressed according to 'the type of girl Malcolm will marry'.

Joseph went to a great deal of trouble to be, without doubt, the most unattractive bride ever to set foot on this planet. His beard had several days' growth, his make-up had trouble matching his eyes. Nevertheless, he arrived in full white bridal outfit, complete with veil. Thank goodness for the veil! My so-called friends, showing the great esteem in which I was held, came in drag, dressed as very unattractive women, one with an expanse of armpit hair, one who was pregnant and one in full Salvation Army uniform, complete with bonnet, who seemed unable to control her fake breasts which kept popping out throughout the evening.

Working in London

I left for London in early 1988. St Thomas' hospital is on the banks of the Thames, immediately opposite Big Ben and the Houses of Parliament. To come to work every day, in the centre of London, and look out over that view is still one of my great memories. Furthermore, it is the hospital where Florence Nightingale worked and nurses who have trained at the hospital can do a postgraduate year, which when completed earns them a Nightingale Badge. It is highly sought after and Nightingale nurses are as well trained as any on the planet. I was fortunate to find a two-bedroom flat in Battersea that had one window that gave a glimpse of the Thames and was only ten minutes' drive from the hospital. Jenni Gowlett, a Salvation Army friend of mine from Australia, was living in London at the time and we agreed to share the rental. We also agreed that Jenni would cook and I would wash up all the dishes. This agreement worked well for us, though I believe I got the best end of the bargain.

There were two plastic surgeons at St Thomas' Hospital—Mr Peter Davis and the younger Mr Bryan Mayou. The registrar who had preceded me was Dr Fiona Wood, now a prominent plastic surgeon in Western Australia, so I had big shoes to fill. At the time I was sporting a moustache and after a few months Peter had told me that as a 33-year-old, brash, single, Australian with a moustache, he initially thought I was gay.

Operating theatres are similar in layout all around the world, so it didn't take me long to get accustomed to the English way of doing things. A few days after I arrived, a new nurse entered the operating theatre. She had chosen theatre as her postgraduate

Nightingale appointment and as I introduced myself to her, I had a strange thought, namely, 'I wonder if this is the lady I will marry?' I am not sure where that came from and my past experience in the operating theatre, where I had fallen in love with a pair of eyes, only to be disappointed when the hat and mask were removed, had me being very cautious, particularly in a new country. I discovered that this nurse was named Fiona and she had an identical twin, also a nurse, and working in one of the St Thomas' wards, where one of my patients was located. Immediately the operating list completed, I went straight to that ward. It was handover time—where nurses handover their patients to the new shift—and any nurse will tell you that any doctor who interrupts handover time takes his life into his own hands. Nevertheless, I was on a mission, so I boldly walked up to the circle of nurses and said, 'Hi, I'm Malcolm Linsell and I would like to do a ward round with…you!' I had looked around the circle, picked out the nurse with the closest features to Fiona and asked her to accompany me to see the patient. The patient was fine, however, for the first time I met Karen, Fiona's twin sister. Thereafter I realised that Fiona was indeed someone I would like to get to know in more depth.

The time at St Thomas' was immensely valuable. I was entrusted to perform more surgical procedures on my own, which included numerous skin grafts and flaps, replanting fingers that had been traumatically separated from the hand and reconstructing breasts that required removal due to breast cancer. One such patient, Kath Stott, was a real fighter. I had reconstructed her breast using a flap and an implant and as I followed her postoperative recovery, I became close to her. After her discharge, we corresponded occasionally and I invited her to visit me in Australia. A few years later when I was back in Melbourne, Kath contacted me again to say she was coming to Melbourne to visit. I was delighted with this and enjoyed taking her around Melbourne. However, she talked very little and it wasn't until we were about to part company, that she told me her breast cancer had spread and that she was dying. Australia was one of the items on her bucket list and I had been honoured to be included in fulfilling her wish to visit and reconnect. Kath died a few months later. There is a story behind every patient. Most often we as doctors don't get to know it. Sometimes, however, we are privileged to discover it and we are the richer for it.

In both the Australian public hospital system and the English NHS system, most plastic surgery is reconstructive. Patients can be admitted to hospital either through the emergency department or after being seen in the outpatient department. Such elective surgical patients are placed on a waiting list depending on the urgency of their case. As would be expected, patients with cancer are given higher priority to those whose conditions are not life threatening. In this way people who are waiting for non-urgent procedures can remain on a waiting list for years. Some people, in spite of being on the waiting list, might never get an operation. It is the registrar's role to manage the waiting list and once the urgent cases are taken care of, it is not uncommon to schedule procedures the registrar would like to see or even perform. One day as I was reviewing the St Thomas' waiting list I discovered a patient who had been waiting for quite a few years. She was scheduled for a meloplasty. A meloplasty is a medical term for a facelift. I was not sure if that was well known to hospital administrators, so, as the urgent and high priority cases for that period had been managed, I thought it would be a good idea to call this lady in for her procedure. I half expected her to be cancelled but to my surprise, she was admitted to hospital and I performed my first facelift (I mean meloplasty) without supervision, under the NHS with no charge to the patient. I wouldn't be surprised if that was the first and only such case ever to occur under the NHS.

Arrogance Begets Mistakes

During this stage of my life, I was still somewhat arrogant and egotistical. During my time at St Thomas' I did two things I regret, which nevertheless, taught me important life lessons. The first occurred when the time came to choose a new Senior House Officer (SHO) to work with me in the plastic surgical unit. As the St Thomas' unit is quite prestigious, there were applications from outstanding young doctors in the UK and throughout Europe. It was left to me to make the final choice. At the time, I was single. Whilst I was keen on Fiona, she was in a relationship, so during the times she was scrubbed for my procedures, I developed a friendship with her, learning about her likes and dislikes, her family and her plans for the future. The fact she had always wanted to travel to Australia I took as a good sign, however, she seemed happy with her boyfriend, so whilst I very much liked her, I held little hope for any future romance.

One of the applicants for the SHO position was Veronique from Paris. She had reasonable references and I pictured her as being straight off the Parisienne catwalks. Veronique got the job. Unfortunately, Veronique did not match the exotic picture I had in my mind. Furthermore, in spite of her keenness, she was also less experienced than many of the other applicants, which meant I had to spend extra time doing some of the jobs that an SHO would do. My arrogance created a situation that was unfair to Veronique and unfair to the other applicants. It served me right and taught me a valuable lesson.

In consideration of job applicants, due
process involves crosschecking facts
and references

My second mistake occurred shortly thereafter. There had been some dialogue with the nurses in theatre about how I had missed the opportunity to defer study for a year, work for six months, then backpack around Europe for six months. However, with Europe just across the English Chanel, I decided to do something similar by taking six weeks off and driving around Europe.

One day in theatre, I was chatting about this and Fiona said, 'Excuse me, Dr Linsell. Would you like a driving partner for your trip around Europe?'

'Well, of course,' I said. Now, sometimes I am not that quick and had to mull over what had just been said.

As soon as the operative procedure finished, I found Fiona outside theatre. 'Fiona, I thought you were in a relationship?' I said.

'I am but I am still my own person,' she said.

'I see. Would you be interested in going out?' I said with my heart in my mouth.

'Sure,' she said as my heart leaped.

'How about tomorrow night?' I said.

'Okay', was her reply.

I am embarrassed to say, that at the time I had an arrogant belief that if someone was not married, then the window of opportunity had not closed with them. I think it is a competition thing with men as it is an ego boost when a woman chooses one man over another.

It is one of my deepest regrets that I did not ensure Fiona had ended her existing relationship or at least had the agreement of her boyfriend before we went out. That our relationship commenced in this way does not sit easily with me. Over the years it has become clear to me that if we don't learn from our past mistakes, we are destined to repeat them or have them repeated on us.

To be in a relationship requires an agreement between two people. Out of respect to all concerned, any change to that agreement needs to be communicated.

Romance Blossoms

Nevertheless, Fiona and I commenced dating and I was clearly keen, because, for our second date, we went to a restaurant in Park Lane, where the menu for Fiona, did not even show the prices. It was also quite helpful to include options such as going to Paris for the weekend during the courting period.

To me, marriage is a lifelong, sacred and solemn commitment between two people. It was a central piece of my Christian upbringing and I was privileged to experience the stability and security that came from that commitment between my mum and dad. Therefore, to ask someone to marry me was a big deal, for I only expected to ask once in my life as my commitment was for ever. Hence, six months after we commenced dating, we were skiing in central Europe. We were staying near Lake Bled, then in Yugoslavia and now in Slovenia. It was early in the year and the lake was frozen over. One night after dinner, I took Fiona for a walk along the shoreline. It was a cold but clear star-filled night, with the 17th-century church floodlit and seemingly raised above the lake. Thus, on the shore of Lake Bled, I got down on one knee and asked Fiona if she would marry me. With me still on one knee, she said several things, none of which included a 'yes'. I therefore had to clarify with her and she did indeed say yes! I was elated. We wanted to tell our parents first, Fiona's were in Salisbury, UK and mine were in New York, so we kept it secret. However, if any of our friends, with whom we were skiing, had been more observant, the damp patch on my right knee was a real giveaway.

I was keen to be married sooner rather than later, however, it was somewhat of a logistical challenge to arrange a wedding at Fiona's home church in Salisbury whilst arranging for people to travel from the UK, USA and Australia. So, once back in London, as a newly engaged couple, we put my car onto one of the ships at Southampton, travelled across the channel to Bayeux, France and commenced the tour of Europe I had been considering for years. One of my friends had warned me that this could be a make or break time for any relationship given we were to spend most of every day in each other's company. However, we had the time of our lives, arriving in Paris or Rome or Salzburg or Berlin with minimal pre-planning and a limited amount of money.

An extended holiday is a great test for a
long-term relationship.

Transformations

Upon our return to the UK, I took up an appointment as plastic surgical registrar at the Mt Vernon Hospital, just outside of London. The hospital had its own dedicated plastic surgical operating theatres with four very experienced consultant plastic surgeons. One of the advantages of working with a large hospital near central London is the fact that it supports more peripheral hospitals around the edge of the CBD. This meant I travelled to other hospitals to conduct outpatient sessions and operate, often without supervision.

By now I felt competent with most plastic surgical procedures, be they reconstructive or cosmetic and the opportunity to improve my consultations with patients along with my surgical technique, in a safe environment, was invaluable. As well as reconstructive procedures, I had the opportunity to perform abdominoplasties and breast reductions so that my training was broad based and thorough.

One incident that had a profound effect on me, concerned a young woman who presented to outpatients requesting a breast augmentation. She was stooped, withdrawn and non-communicative. Attempting to discuss the pros and cons of the procedure with her was challenging, for she seemed to acknowledge little of what was said. Examining her was nigh on impossible and we considered whether she might not be suitable for the procedure. Nevertheless, we decided to proceed and the operation was uneventful. Six weeks later, she returned to out patients. She was totally transformed. She was dressed stylishly, shoulders back, her hair back off her face and as she walked in, exuded a confidence I had no idea could have emanated from the same woman. This was a revelation for me, as for the first time, I saw the positive impact surgery could have to improve a person's appearance and could have on a person's whole demeanour. It was the increase in confidence that was most striking and I have now seen this time and time and time again.

A change in appearance can have a
dramatic effect on the way a person feels
about themselves.

On 1 July 1989, Fiona and I married, in front of our parents, extended family and friends at the Church of England Parish Church in West Harnham. Fiona had threatened to walk to the church so I organised for her to be transported by horse and carriage. She looked radiant and I was so happy. One attendee from Australia was Dr Joe Marich. Thank goodness he had discarded his bridal regalia for more conservative and traditional attire. My best man was my brother Derek with my groomsman Dr Stephen Cobb.

I kept the location of the honeymoon secret from Fiona. I did, however, suggest she should pack for somewhere warm. From Salisbury we were driven to the Grand Hotel in Brighton (which was bombed by the IRA in 1984) for our first night as a married couple, then transferred to Heathrow the next morning for the flight to the Caribbean. The first week was spent on one of the islands. For the second week I had hired our own yacht, complete with skipper and cook, and sailed in between the islands lapping up the sun, crystal clear water and magnificent local produce.

Dr Stephen Cobb, my groomsman, was the bandmaster of the International Staff Band (ISB) of the Salvation Army as well as the Hendon Salvation Army Band. Soon after arriving in England, I had attended worship at the Hendon Corps. Steve and his wife, Elaine, had invited my flatmate Jenni and I to lunch. We kept going for Sunday lunch for the next two years! Steve was a brilliant cornet player and an outstanding leader of men. The ISB is recognised as the pre-eminent band in the Salvation Army and its high standards have been maintained and exceeded under Steve's leadership. Steve invited me to play in the Hendon band, one of England's foremost corps bands. I jumped at the chance and loved playing in another outstanding band, with highlights including performing concerts in the Royal Festival Hall and playing on a couple of recordings.

When Steve asked me to fill in for one of the ISB solo cornet players who had become ill, I was over the moon. I was a member of the band when we recorded in the Abbey Road studios (the same studios made famous by the Beatles). Once again, I got to play in the Royal Albert Hall, this time as a member of the ISB. What a thrill.

Not bad for one who, 30 years previously, had started his playing career in the back of a VW Kombi in Burnie, Tasmania.

Back to Australia

In early 1990, after a little over two years in England, it was time to return to Australia with a new bride. At the same time, my brother Lieutenant Derek Linsell was appointed to open the Salvation Army's work in Cranbourne, about 43km from Berwick, south-east of Melbourne. Derek had to recruit his own team and commencing with nothing, attract a congregation to a church that was yet to exist. Derek is creative, charismatic and was totally committed to the task ahead. He asked Fiona and I to join the team and we readily accepted. This for me was a major departure from what had been the norm. For the first time in about 30 years, I was no longer playing in a brass band and I no longer needed to practise the cornet. I relished the extra time I had in the day, however, it is impossible to replace the camaraderie and connection that exists in a Salvation Army brass band.

Derek was tireless in his efforts and, to his and the team's credit, 100 people attended our first church service. Derek occasionally saw rules as guidelines and the Cranbourne Salvation Army became an alternative to the more traditional forms of worship found in other churches. Derek wanted worship to be fun and entertaining, so when I was appointed to lead the worship, he gave me full reign. When the Salvation Army commenced in 1865, its founder, William Booth, was not averse to thinking outside the box to attract people to church. I thought it might be a good idea to write Christian lyrics to well known songs. I spent quite a bit of time in the car driving between my rooms and various hospitals, so I would listen to my favourite songs in the car and write new lyrics as I drove along. In this way the congregation got to sing songs from Michael Jackson, Rod Stewart, John Lennon, ABBA, The Beatles, The Corrs and so on. I had a lot of fun and the congregation also seemed to enjoy it.

Meanwhile, one of my priorities was passing the second part of the surgical exam, which would allow me to commence practice as a plastic surgeon. The exam comprised a written component as well as several oral examinations in anatomy, pathology and plastic surgery. I had studied intermittently whilst at Mt Vernon, however, hit the books full-time when I returned to Melbourne. The exam was held in Sydney over a period of four days. When I attended my anatomy oral exam, one of my examiners, was Mr John Hanrahan who more than 20 years previously, had inspired me to follow in his footsteps. He, of course, knew none of this. He produced a skull and over the next 20 minutes asked me detailed questions about the various skull orifices and their relationship to nerves and blood vessels. I was hopelessly, inadequately prepared for the detailed knowledge required. I was not surprised, when a few days later the candidates gathered at the College of Surgeons for the results, my name was not one of those read out. The failure deeply impacted me. I felt embarrassed and inadequate. I was on the precipice of entering my chosen profession and I had fallen well short.

As with the first part, a candidate can keep sitting the second part until a pass is attained. The next scheduled exam was in early October. I took up assisting again to gain some well-needed income while Fiona worked as a scrub nurse at one of the local private hospitals. My theoretical knowledge was reasonable, however, it did not stand up to the rigours of an oral examination. Whilst I was assisting Murray Stapleton, he would drill me with plastic surgical questions and scenarios. I also returned to my old anatomy school at Monash University to learn the various anatomical structures in more detail. As I no longer had access to a fresh human cadaver, I would study prospected specimens found in Perspex containers.

For a more hands on experience, the anatomy department kept large vats of various body parts, immersed in formalin. These parts could rarely be seen from the surface so we would don large rubber gloves that extended above the elbow, to feel around in the tank and retrieve various specimens to study. Unfortunately, some of the tanks were deeper than arms length and it was not unusual to be reaching down deep into a tank and have formalin containing various pieces of body parts, flood in above the glove. This is not an experience I can recommend!

Nevertheless, when I sat the next exam over the days leading up to the AFL Grand Final, I was better prepared. The anatomy oral exam had gone reasonably smoothly. On the Saturday, Grand Final Day, I had my clinical exam, which comprised a long case (spending 20 minutes with a patient with a complex plastic surgical problem, then presenting my findings and treatment plan to the examiners) and several short cases. The long case had gone well, then in one of my short cases I made an error that I would expect even a medical student to get right.

I knew I had failed, even before the gathering at the College to hear the results. For the second time, it was a crushing blow.

I had a standing room ticket to the Melbourne Cricket Ground to watch the Grand Final between Collingwood and Essendon. My brother Derek, to his absolute credit, saw how pathetic I must have looked and swapped his prized seat in the grand stand for my standing room ticket. Collingwood had not won the flag for 32 years, having nine unsuccessful attempts in the meantime. They were ridiculed for having 'the colliwobbles,' However, on this day, led by their captain and Norm Smith medallist (for best player on the field) Tony Shaw, Collingwood emphatically won by 48 points. On the day, I had trouble focusing on the game, however, in the Monday newspaper, there was a full-page picture of Tony Shaw leading his team onto the ground at the commencement of the match. I was fascinated by the look on his face. To me it said, 'We are going to win today, and nothing and nobody will stand in our way!' That was the attitude I needed for the next time I sat the exam.

Determination to Succeed

I am told that one of the definitions of insanity is doing the same thing and expecting a different result. For me to become a plastic surgeon, I needed a different plan of action. Firstly, I put Tony Shaw's photo above my study desk because I wanted his attitude. I was passing the next time and nothing and nobody would stand in my way. The next thing I did was change my study technique. Up until then, I had worked primarily alone. That had to change. I knew three other Melbourne trainees who were sitting the next exam scheduled for Brisbane in mid 1991. I set up a study group and invited them to our place every week for us to work together in team. Furthermore, I rang some examiners, who had positions at major hospitals in Melbourne, to ask if I could attend their out patient sessions. They were happy to help and so I exposed myself to constant questioning under conditions not dissimilar to those of the exams. One word of advice one of them gave me was very telling. It was this. 'At the examination, we are not looking for trainees, we are looking for plastic surgeons. When you come across as one of our colleagues, rather than a student, then you will become just that!' That is some of the best advice I have ever been given.

In late 1990, we discovered that Fiona was pregnant with our first child. The birth was due a few weeks after the exam. This created a significant degree of extra pressure, for with a new baby, I would be the sole generator of income.

When the time of the examination arrived I was ready. I knew my knowledge was more than adequate, I knew my surgical technique was good and now I knew I was ready to become a plastic surgeon. During the oral clinical examinations, I was respectful, yet confident and clear. This was true also in anatomy and pathology.

When a heavily pregnant Fiona and I mixed with our friends for the announcement of the results, my quiet confidence was mixed with a degree of anxiety. The results are announced by the head examiner inviting the people whose names are read out to join the examiners behind closed doors for celebratory drinks. If your name is not read out, you slink away to hit the books for another six months. That had been my experience the past two times and it was not something I wanted to repeat.

The names are read out in alphabetical order. One of our study group members name started with 'C'. His name was called. Great news. Linsell is in the middle of the alphabet. It seemed to take forever to get down to the 'L's. And then, 'Malcolm Linsell' was read out. Wow! I had done it. I had *finally* done it! Fiona and I embraced. A dream that had started as a 6-year-old boy, and taken 30 years to fulfil, was about to become a reality. It was an unbelievable sense of fulfilment and achievement overcoming the disappointment of past failures, to finally attain something so worthwhile. I felt very, very fortunate. As an added bonus, each member of our four-member Melbourne study team passed at the same time. Melbourne was about to have four brand new plastic surgeons.

If a goal is achievable, a single-minded determination with a good dose of resilience will usually see it realised.

Malcolm Linsell, Plastic Surgeon

I commenced practice in plastic surgery in Melbourne on Monday, 3 June 1991. On Wednesday 5 June 1991, our first child, Rebekah Kate Linsell (Bek) was born. I was besotted…and still am. She was so beautiful…and still is.

I was appointed to the Dandenong and District Hospital, a very busy public hospital serving the south-east of Melbourne. Mr Simon Donahoe was the head of the unit and was enormously supportive of me. I had worked with Simon at the Alfred, then the VPSU, then the Peter MacCallum Cancer Centre. He was an excellent teacher, explaining and demonstrating the techniques that he had developed over time. He was also an outstanding human being. He and his wife Paula were the proud parents of eight children and he always found a balance between plastic surgery and life that I found refreshing. Simon had recently commenced partnership with Mr Michael Leung, a young plastic surgeon gifted in microsurgery. I had trained with Michael at the VPSU. Michael was patient and tireless, able to maintain his high standards at all hours of the day and night. For a time, Michael and I did most of the on-call emergency work at the Dandenong hospital. I also made myself available for the on-call emergency work at the Dandenong Valley Private Hospital, so as the months went by my practice grew. In providing a great service to patients requiring emergency treatment (lacerated or crushed hands or fingers, facial injuries, burns) the patients would often tell their friends and GPs. It was not long until I began seeing patients requesting treatment for skin cancer and hand deformities as well as cosmetic surgery. When I first commenced practice, there was still a Medicare Item number for breast augmentation, however, breast reduction and abdominoplasty were more common procedures.

In the early stage of practice our home telephone number was given to patients. Fiona was not unknown to be feeding Bek with one hand and making patient appointments by phone with the other. We had only one car, so I would often be dropped off at the hospital, while Fiona took Bek to her postnatal appointments, then later picked me up from the hospital. It was also not unusual, if we were both working in the operating theatre, for Bek to be in her car seat, in the corner of theatre. As time went on, the patients got to know Bek, following her development and asking after her if she wasn't with us at the time.

At that time, the suburb of Berwick was one of the fastest growing areas in Australia. (It still is.) I decided it would be an ideal location for my first set of rooms. Initially I shared rooms with a general surgeon then after a few months, approached a young dentist, Dr Paris Kritharides, to see if he would be interested in having a plastic surgeon consulting from one of his rooms. He was, and I consulted from Paris's rooms for over a year, before moving into my own rooms in Berwick.

1993 was a big year. On 18 January our son, Timothy Luke Linsell, was born. I was so happy to have both a daughter and a son. Bek and Tim are the greatest joys of my life and I am so privileged to be their dad. Tim was born by elective caesarean section, which is just as well, as his umbilical chord was around his neck. If he had been born with a normal delivery, the chord would have strangled him, causing foetal distress and an emergency caesarean section. Interestingly, with Fiona's first pregnancy the obstetrician was emphatic that with a nurse and plastic surgeon as parents a caesarean section was the preferred method of delivery. The day after Tim was born, I was taking 19-month-old Bek in to see her new baby brother. I was driving and she was in her car seat in the rear of the car. It had been a busy day, I had not eaten and it was quite a long drive to the hospital. I called into the local McDonald's to pick up dinner, which included my favourite chocolate thick shake. I handed my thick shake back to Bek, asking her to hold it for me until I was

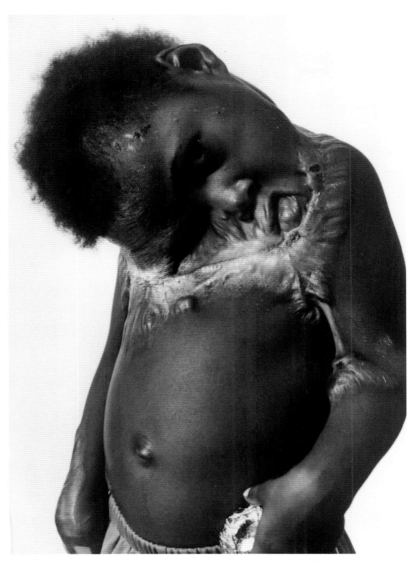

Wesley, pre-op April 1993, showing his head at 90 degrees to his body.

Wesley, post-op in his compression garments and head brace to help him keep his head straight.

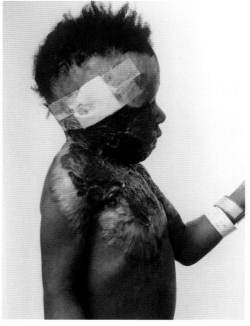

Wesley, six months after his first operation.

The first time Wesley and I had seen each other in 20 years.

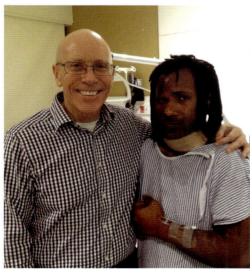

The day after Wesley's last operation at St Vincent's Private Hospital in Kew.

Karl Stefanovic, keeping us all amused while filming in Goroka, PNG, with Chick Davey on sound.

The whole team who contributed to the story in Goroka, PNG.
Photograph by Stephen Taylor.

Wesley reunited with his mum and dad.

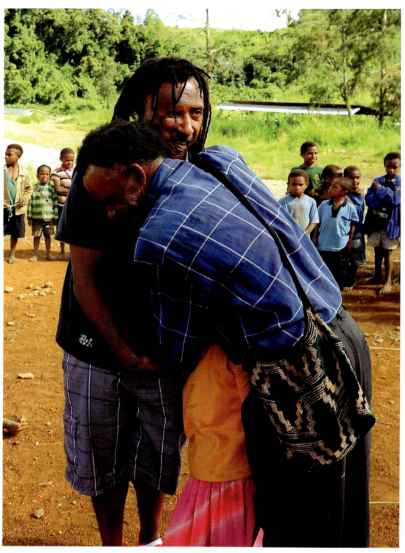

Wesley sees his dad, Koni, for the first time in more than ten years.

PNG tribesmen in Goroka, PNG.

Wesley's village, Onamuga in Eastern Highlands Province, PNG.

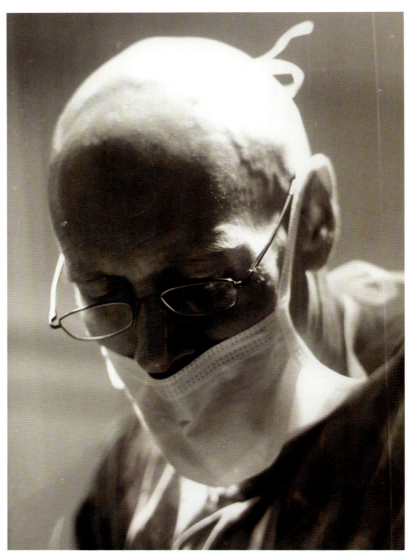

One of my favourite shots, taken whilst operating by my anaesthetist, Dr Joe Marich.

ready to drink it. A few minutes later, I put my hand back to retrieve my shake and it was not forthcoming. I looked at Bek in the rear-vision mirror to find chocolate shake all around her mouth with her smiling and giggling. I went hungry and she finished the lot.

During my time in London, on an intermittent basis, I had continued to write up my thesis. Whilst performing microsurgery on rats had been fun, tabulating the results, sourcing references, preparing photographs and writing the prose can be quite tedious. In 1992, I made a concerted effort to spend my spare time writing and collating. When it was finally complete, the volume was bound and submitted to Monash University for assessment. Although it was unlikely to win a Nobel Prize, I felt a major sense of achievement just in submitting it. It was the completion of my research and an unexpectedly enjoyable two years of my life. In 1993 Monash University awarded me a Masters of Surgery (MS) of which I was quite proud, for at that time, few plastic surgeons in Australia had attained the degree.

In 1993 The Salvation Army publication, *The War Cry*, asked if I would feature in an article they would prepare. I am not sure there are too many other Salvation Army bandsman in the world who have become plastic surgeons, so they thought a story about why I was doing what I did, would be of interest to their readers. When the article was published it was a front-page story with a photograph of Fiona and I in the operating theatre, with the headlines, 'Everybody has the right to walk tall and feel good about themselves.' The article went on to explain how I loved what I did because, by restoring or improving a person's physical appearance, confidence was restored and this was infectious.

When a person feels good about
themselves, everybody around
them benefits.

The readership of *The War Cry* is somewhat limited to Salvation Army people, and people in the pub, who might buy a copy and rarely read it. I wasn't to suspect, that one reader in the Eastern Highlands province of Papua New Guinea (PNG) was to have a major impact on the life of a little boy she knew, as well as on my own life.

Wesley

Lorraine Mack was a nurse and Salvation Army Captain from Sydney. She was stationed at the medical clinic of a small village named Onamuga in the Eastern Highlands Province of PNG. The village is remote and only accessed by a tortuous dirt road or by helicopter. One day, a little boy aged three or four, was rushed to the clinic. The story was that he had been ill, lying on a bench and being tended to by his mother in their hut. The fire in the centre of the hut was burning fiercely to keep the little boy warm. The little boy's elder brother was playing outside the hut and cried out, alarming his mother. The little boy was momentarily left unattended by his mother as she went outside to attend to her other young child. In that moment, the little boy rolled off the bench, straight into the fire. He was too ill to struggle free. His head, face, chest and right hand caught alight and had burned deeply into his flesh before his frantic mother returned, patted out the flames and rushed him to the clinic. The little boy's name was Wesley Koni.

Over the next few days, Wesley was treated at the clinic with the limited facilities available, however, the extent of the burns was so great it was decided to transfer him to the regional hospital at Goroka. Information on how he was treated at Goroka is limited, however, it would appear that Wesley spent extended periods with his head flopping onto his chest. He lost his right ear and all the fingers of his right hand.

When Wesley eventually returned to Onamuga, his wounds were healed but his head was now fused with his chest, his right hand was little more than a club and his mouth was attached to the left side of his chest. Feeding him was an issue as food needed to be spooned in from the level of his chest.

Lorraine knew that Wesley would be a burden to the tribe and it was likely he would die unless there was some sort of intervention. As she was contemplating this, she read an article in *The War Cry* on a Salvationist plastic surgeon in Melbourne who thought everybody had the right to feel good about themselves.

Somehow Lorraine got hold of my email address, wrote an impassioned letter and sent photographs of Wesley. I had not seen anything quite like it, however, I thought there might be something I could do. I contacted my brother Derek and showed him the photographs. Without question, he felt the young church of Cranbourne Salvation Army should come together to make a difference in this little boy's life.

Derek contacted Colin Smith, one of the church members, to lead the logistical team. Colin was a big man with an even bigger heart. He is one of the greatest organisers I have ever known and he took on Wesley as a lifelong project. I contacted Lorraine and told her that we were willing to help and that 'Operation Wesley' had been launched. Colin and his team got to work to organise the logistics of transporting Wesley and his father Koni, from the remote highlands of PNG to Melbourne.

Meanwhile, I felt this might be a story that would be of interest to television viewers. I knew Wesley would be a long-term project so sharing it with a nightly current affairs program did not seem to suit. Instead I contacted Channel 9's *60 Minutes* and was eventually put in touch with a producer named, Stephen Taylor. Whilst still reasonably young, Stephen had worked on the show for about eight years, so he knew what would make a good story. Interestingly, Stephen's father was well known in PNG having been the CEO of EM TV for several years. Stephen felt the story would be of interest and when the operation was scheduled, he promised to be there along with a cameraman and sound engineer.

It was an enormous logistical feat for Wesley and his father Koni to travel from the primitive village of Onamuga in PNG to Melbourne, Australia and then to Cranbourne. That in itself is a major tribute to Lorraine, Colin and their teams. Koni had never been outside his village, he spoke no English and his son did not leave his arms the whole time. Koni demonstrated enormous courage, determination and love for his son.

Wesley and Koni arrived late at night. Nothing could have prepared me. I communicated with Koni through a translator. Wesley was terrified and clung to his father, so examining him was not that easy. It was clear Wesley would require multiple surgeries, however, the most important and the one that carried the most risk, was to separate his head from his chest.

When a movable area of the body is burned then heals with a scar, movement is restricted because the scar tissue is firm and inflexible. The treatment principle is quite simple. It requires incising the scar tissue and stretching out the movable parts. This leaves a raw area, which requires a skin graft (a thin slice of skin taken from elsewhere on the body) to cover it. The skin graft is placed on the raw area in such a way that blood vessels grow from the raw surface into the new skin so that the new skin 'takes'. If the skin doesn't take the body makes even more scar tissue. This operation is called a 'release and graft of burns scar contracture'. At the age of 13, I had undergone the same operation to release the scar on my right hand. However, the operation for Wesley required a great deal more planning and carried a significantly higher risk.

There are major blood vessels on each side of the neck carrying blood from the heart to the brain. These are accompanied by major nerves. My main concern with Wesley was that we didn't know how close these vessels were to the surface of the skin or if they were caught up in the scar tissue. If they were, an incision into the scar tissue might damage the blood vessels resulting in life threatening bleeding.

Dr Bill Shearer was a first class anaesthetist I had been working with. We had both commenced practice around the same time and I had full confidence Wesley was in safe hands with Bill. When Bill saw Wesley, he was concerned with Wesley's neck. When a patient is asleep under general anaesthetic, the anaesthetist places a plastic tube down their throat into their windpipe in order to supply oxygen to the lungs. Bill was concerned, because Wesley's neck was twisted, so he might not be able to put a tube into Wesley's windpipe. Nevertheless, we decided we could handle that eventuality.

I next took Wesley to see a couple of my more experienced plastic surgical colleagues for their advice. Even with their decades of experience, they also had not seen anything like the extent of Wesley's scars. They had little further to offer other than a pat on the back and wished me well.

My plastic surgical colleague, Mr Michael Leung agreed to assist me at the operation. This meant a lot to me for Michael's clear-headed and wise decision making would make my job so much easier. Brenda Linsell, my sister-in-law with a wealth of operating theatre experience, offered to be the scrub nurse. The operating team was outstanding!

The Dandenong and District Hospital very generously offered the use of their facilities to look after Wesley. This was so important.

The operating theatres were first class and, postoperatively, Wesley would be managed in the intensive care unit. It was comforting to know Wesley was being cared for by an outstanding medical team in a world-class facility.

It was time to bring it together.

The operation was scheduled for a Saturday morning. The day before, the *60 Minutes* team (Stephen Taylor, producer, Dennis Nicholson, cameraman and Geoff Spurrell, sound engineer) spent time with Wesley to gain preoperative footage. As yet a reporter had not been assigned to the story. For Wes and I to be interviewed, Stephen would ask the questions for me to respond. At this stage Wesley would sit on my knee, however, he was very suspicious of me. His communication with me and also with the camera was negligible.

The First Operation

On the Saturday morning, the whole team assembled early. Geoff placed a microphone on my scrubs and I would remain connected in this way for the whole procedure. That, in itself, is a little scary. If things are going well, answering questions and making commentary is not too difficult. It is a different story if things are not going to plan. If this were to happen the cameras would keep rolling. Sometimes the pictures alone tell the story and sound can be inserted at a later date.

I will never forget Wesley's cry as Dr Bill Shearer, the anaesthetist, carried him into theatre. Put yourself in Wesley's shoes for a moment. Surrounded by big white people, none of whom spoke his language, in totally unfamiliar surroundings, separated from his dad, perhaps for the first time ever and knowing that whatever was going to happen was going to hurt like crazy!

Bill was able to get access to a vein to give Wesley some sedation. However, several attempts to insert a tube into his windpipe, even using sophisticated techniques, were unsuccessful. Wesley's airway was kinked at a 90-degree angle. It is amazing that he was able to breathe by himself when conscious. To proceed with such a large operation without control of the airway was out of the question. An alternative plan was required and it was required immediately.

Michael, Bill and I decided to separate Wesley's head from his chest under local anaesthetic and sedation. With this done, Bill could then give a general anaesthetic and insert the tube into his windpipe.

Separating Wesley's head and neck from his chest was always the riskiest part of the operation due to the potential damage to the major blood vessels of his neck. If this occurred there was potentially a catastrophic bleed. (This is where I was grateful for the training in vascular surgery at the Alfred as well as working with Michael, one of Australia's best microvascular surgeons.)

The surgical team was scrubbed and ready. We prepared Wesley's skin with antiseptic and covered the rest of his body with sterile drapes. Most plastic surgeons draw on the skin before making an incision. Whether we use that drawing or not is another thing, for Mr Don Marshal, a plastic surgical mentor, used to tell me it was only a guideline anyway! For Wesley, I had drawn a line horizontally across his neck and injected local anaesthetic containing adrenaline. The local anaesthetic prevented him feeling pain, while the adrenaline constricts blood vessels and reduces the amount of bleeding in the skin. However, it would have little effect if a major blood vessel was cut. With Wesley sedated, but not asleep, it was important this part of the operation proceeded as quickly as possible. Bill was holding a mask on Wesley's face so there was limited space to move.

I made the first incision, the full length of his neck. The scar was thick and firm, more than 5mm thick in some sections. It took several passes of the knife to get through it but as soon as we did, we reached healthy subcutaneous tissue. With Wesley's head under stretch, his face started to separate from his chest. It is one of the most startling things I have seen in my surgical career. As we incised and gently broke through the scar tissue, into healthy tissue beneath the skin, Wesley's face, neck and head were separated from his chest, for the first time in a few years. And most importantly, no major blood vessels or nerves were on show or damaged.

We kept going for the scar tissue extended to Wesley's right shoulder. As Wesley's head finally separated from his body, we found a hole, which was now the only remaining remnant of Wesley's right ear. By the time this was complete, Wesley's head and neck were now fully extended leaving a large raw area on the right side of his face, neck and upper part of his chest, about 25 per cent of his body surface. It was bleeding but that was easily controlled. Most importantly, we could all breathe a sigh of relief, for his major vessels were intact. With Wesley's head extended, Bill could then place a tube into his windpipe (trachea), securing his airway. It was only at that stage we were satisfied we had things under control and we could all relax a little. During elective surgery, it seems strange to say it, but for the most part the work is routine and the surgical teams are relaxed. There will often be lighthearted banter between various members of the team, which will help to pass the time. However, if a surgeon, assistant, scrub nurse or anaesthetist loses concentration for a moment, things can quickly change.

The 25 per cent of Wesley's body that had now been exposed required coverage with a skin graft to enable it to heal. This is accomplished by slicing a thin layer of skin from one area of the body and using it to cover the defect. The donor site (the site from which the skin is taken) is covered with a dressing and heals of its own accord over about ten days. It heals in the same way a graze on the body heals. For those who have grazed their knee, they will know this is painful. Imagine all the skin from your lower abdomen and both legs (front and back), taken at the same time. It would be excruciating. Wesley was a small boy, so to find enough skin to cover the raw area that had been made, this is what was required. Harvesting a skin graft is a fine art in itself. It uses a very sharp, long blade, with a guard that has to be set to cut at just the right depth for the skin. If the depth is too thin, the skin fragments. If the depth is too thick, a full thickness piece of skin is removed and this takes too long to heal. It is a little like the same motion used for slicing the Christmas ham. As the skin comes away, the scrub nurse retrieves it and lays it on a special *tulle gras* dressing before it is stitched on to the recipient site.

The operation took about three hours. It had gone as well as could be expected. The surgical team had been calm and efficient. The *60 Minutes* team, who were still standing despite the quite confronting surgical procedure, seemed happy with the footage. This was just as well, for we were unlikely to do a second take. I found out later that this was Stephen Taylor's first trip to the operating theatre, so for him it was one to remember.

When I visited Wesley the following day, I knew we had a problem. His pain was well controlled, however, even with the dressings in place, his head had fallen down and was resting on his chest. His head was too heavy for his withered neck muscles to lift it back into a normal position. This was not something I had anticipated. What was needed was something to support his head while his neck muscles were regaining their strength. Enter a very gifted occupational therapist named Kristin who was able to fashion a splint that sat on his shoulders and held his head up. This would have been very uncomfortable for Wesley, however, throughout this period, he demonstrated enormous courage. Although it was challenging to communicate with him, somehow he knew that our intention was to do our best for him.

A week after the first procedure, the good news was his skin grafts were healing well. One of the concerns with healing skin grafts is that the gaps between the new skin can become thick and raised which might lead to keloid scarring. A person with black skin is more at risk of this occurring. Kristin arranged for some head to toe compression garments to be made for Wesley to wear. He lived in these for months and was very cute as he proudly displayed Thomas the Tank Engine on his chest.

The fact Wesley did so well at the first operation is a tribute to dozens of people, many working behind the scenes, who responded to a little boy's need and did what they could. People responded with their hearts and a little boy was given the opportunity to embrace a life vastly different to the one he would have otherwise had. This, to me, is one of the greatest facets of human nature.

When people give abundantly, in order to make a difference, they receive back far more than they have given.

Operation Wesley required several return trips to Australia for Wesley to undergo many more operations. These were all organised by Colin and his superb team and funded by The Salvation Army and the local communities of Cranbourne and Berwick.

As Wesley grew, the original skin grafts did not grow with him, so he required more operations and more grafts to allow him to maintain his movement. Amazingly, the original donor sites from his legs healed so well, we were able to reuse them as graft donor sites. However, every time more grafts were taken, more pain was inflicted. Not once did Wesley refuse a procedure. His courage and determination have always been inspirational.

After a few years, Wesley was outgrowing his skin grafts. It became time for more sophisticated measures to be used to give him more permanent relief. I asked my colleague Mr Michael Leung if he would take over Wesley's management. Michael's reputation and expertise in microvascular surgery was outstanding and he and his team performed several surgeries. A major breakthrough was achieved when Michael took a free flap of tissue from Wesley's back and inserted this into the front of Wesley's neck. This tissue was flexible and pliable, which meant Wesley gained movement of his head rather than being restricted by inflexible scar tissue.

Because the *60 Minutes* team had been present from the start and filmed countless hours of footage I expected the story to go to air at some stage. This never happened and I was always curious why this was the case. Nevertheless, to us, the most important thing was that Wesley had come through and was thriving. This had made it all worthwhile.

Over the next few years, things were changing. When Derek left the Cranbourne Salvation Army, we decided it would be better to attend the Baptist church, which was just around the corner from our house, rather than travel the forty minutes to Cranbourne. The people at the Ashburton Baptist church were very welcoming and I relished the freedom that came with less responsibility. I did, however, lead worship occasionally and to their credit the parishioners coped well with me singing 'Wake up Christian' to the music of Rod Stuart's 'Maggie May'!

Part Five

Building a Career...Then Giving It Away

The Road Not Taken

I have always been an avid reader of books, both fiction and non-fiction. One of my favourite authors is M Scott Peck. His book *The Road Less Travelled*, had a profound impact on me. I identified with the words from Robert Frost's poem, entitled *The Road Not Taken* and have used them often.

> *Two roads diverged in a wood, and I—*
> *I took the one less travelled by,*
> *And that has made all the difference.*

Rather than follow everybody else moving along a well-trodden path, I tend to want to do things differently. Occasionally, that means finding or creating a way that hadn't existed before. Sometimes, the desire to be different has led to choices that have been very costly, physically, mentally and emotionally. However, through all of life's experiences I can honestly say, it is those choices that have made all the difference.

Early in my practice, I coined the term, 'Surgery of Self-Esteem' when referring to cosmetic surgery. I had consistently seen the difference a tummy tuck or breast reduction or facelift had on an individual. For instance, children who are born with prominent ears, are often teased mercilessly by other children and believe it or not, adults as well. They are called, 'Big Ears', 'Wing Nuts', 'Dumbo' and other derogatory names. Children respond by withdrawing, growing their hair long or not going swimming in order to avoid the teasing. A simple operation called an otoplasty—correction of prominent ears—pins the ears back to a normal position in relation the head and the teasing stops immediately, for there is nothing to tease. This is a cosmetic procedure. If nothing is done, the ears still function normally. It is an operation designed to improve a person's appearance and hence the way they feel about themselves. (It is occasionally performed on adults whose parents have prevented them from having an operation as a child.) To my mind this is no different from an abdominoplasty, a breast reduction or even a facelift or breast augmentation. Each of these procedures changes the physical appearance and can have a dramatic positive impact on the way people feel about themselves. When people feel good about themselves, they feel more confident. Confidence is attractive. Confident people are more fun to be around.

Some people consider cosmetic surgery to be vain. Some patients would express concern that they would be seen to be vain. This is rarely the case and I would reassure patients that in my experience, vanity is about comparing yourself with others; considering yourself better than others or wanting to be better than others. Wanting to feel good about yourself and be more confident, is not vanity.

I enjoyed cosmetic surgery. I was good at it. I had an eye for it, being able to visualise results and explain what was possible to a patient, in a way that was honest and reassuring. Mostly they were grateful. Those who were not could be very challenging.

It is interesting that it is the small number of challenging patients that can change the way all patients are managed. For instance, early in my practice I did not take funds prior to the operation. That was until I performed a facelift on a middle-aged man who did not keep his follow-up appointment to have his sutures removed or to pay his fee. Thereafter, all fees were paid upfront.

I enjoyed managing patients with skin cancer as well. They were different for they required long-term follow up and often developed further lesions that required treatment. As I saw them regularly over a period of years, I got to know them and they me. In the majority of instances, skin cancer that is treated early can be cured. However, some skin cancers, particularly melanomas, can be aggressive and spread throughout the body rapidly, usually with fatal results. Losing a patient to cancer was one of the distressing parts of practice, as I had often got to know them and their families.

One patient I remember well was named Karen Hawkins. Karen was in her early twenties and was referred to me with a pigmented lesion on her scalp. This was a suspected melanoma and was concerning in one so young, however, a major complicating factor was that Karen was pregnant with her second child. Pregnancy has been known to rapidly increase the spread of melanoma, which can not only kill the mother, but the unborn child as well. When a woman is pregnant, it is best to delay any anaesthetic until at least the second trimester (after 13 weeks) to lessen the chance of harm to the developing foetus. However, a diagnosis of melanoma changes everything. The first thing to do was confirm the diagnosis. This was done with a small procedure and shortly thereafter, the diagnosis of melanoma was confirmed. Melanoma can cause damage by either recurring adjacent to the original lesion or spreading to other locations in the body. Melanomas require a wider re-excision of the scar to lessen the chance of 'local recurrence'. I discussed all the pros and cons with Karen and her husband, Scott. Although Karen was in the early stages of her pregnancy, we decided to do a further procedure under general anaesthetic in order to perform a wider procedure. In the vast majority of cases, this is all that is required. Karen and baby came through the procedure well, however, we were both dismayed when the pathology report said that the melanoma had been incompletely excised. We again discussed the options. Karen required a further procedure, which meant she would remove most of her hair-bearing scalp with some of the underlying bone of her skull. Furthermore, it might be necessary for her pregnancy to be terminated. This was now out of my area of expertise and I referred Karen to my colleague Mr Michael Leung and the Victorian Melanoma Unit. Karen and I kept in contact for a while but we then lost contact and I feared the worst.

In the mid 1990s I was looking for a procedure to focus on in order to offer a premium service. At that time, abdominoplasties (tummy tucks) were performed with little finesse. They were often apronectomies, which improved an overhanging abdomen but little was done to improve the shape. In fact, many plastic surgeons were wary of abdominoplasty for their relatively high risk of complications. A surgeon I respected greatly, Mr Peter Davis, one of my mentors from St Thomas' Hospital, had said to me, that 'of all the procedures you do, abdominoplasty will give you the most problems!' Liposuction was seen to be too risky to combine with an abdominoplasty for it was said that it dramatically increased the rate of wound breakdown.

Women who present for an abdominoplasty are usually post pregnancy. They have often had flat tummies in their twenties, however, after one and particularly after two children, the muscle which runs down either side of the midline, has been split apart to make way for the growing baby. This is what contributes to most of the bulge and no amount of sit-ups can correct it. Combine this with loose, floppy skin and bulges of fat that seem resistant to diet and exercise, back pain and continence issues, and you have a post pregnancy tummy that women hate with a passion. What they are looking for is a flatter, tighter and more shapely tummy. With the techniques that were available at the time, we could sometimes achieve flatter and tighter but rarely improve the shape during the one procedure.

When I read about the work of the late Dr Ted Lockwood in one of the American plastic surgical journals, I was intrigued. He had developed a safe technique whereby he could combine liposuction with an abdominoplasty and his published results were phenomenal. His technique for the first time presented the possibility of safely achieving a flatter, tighter, more shapely tummy in the one procedure. This is what I had been looking for. If I could learn and perfect this technique, I could offer a service that few others in Australia were offering.

I studied the technique and little by little began to apply it with my patients. The first time I combined liposuction with an abdominoplasty I was a little tense. It was quite possible that it would be disastrous with the abdominal skin dying and the wound falling apart. At the end of the procedure, I checked the skin and all seemed well. I checked it that evening at the end of the list, before I went home, then had a fairly anxious night half expecting a call from the nursing staff to say the skin of the abdomen was going black. This did not happen and when I checked tummy the next morning, the skin was healthy and all was well. This was quite a revelation for me and dramatically improved the possibility for better results with tummy-tuck procedures.

In time, as I performed a few more cases I became more confident with the amount of liposuction I could perform. Consequently, my results from suction-assisted abdominoplasty far exceeded those

I had previously. I felt that I should share my experience with my colleagues and elected to present my first major paper to my colleagues at the Australian and American Societies of Aesthetic Plastic Surgeon's meeting at Port Douglas. I had presented papers before, however, this was the first time I was showing a new technique to my colleagues, most of whom were vastly more experienced than I. Whilst I was confident of my results, I wanted the presentation to be entertaining. I had been told that if you start any presentation with a joke, you are more likely to have the attention of the audience. I was watching *The Footy Show* one night and Trevor Marmalade told a joke that made everyone laugh. I borrowed it for the start of my presentation. It went something like this:

> *Ladies and gentlemen, as I stand before you today,*
> *I feel a little like the man who was caught in*
> *bed with another man's wife when the husband*
> *returned home. The husband was a big, burly bloke*
> *who angrily grabbed the perpetrator by the scruff*
> *of the neck and frog-marched him out to the tool-*
> *shed at the back of the house. He then secured the*
> *terrified man's member in a vice and produced a*
> *hacksaw blade. 'Crikey mate. You are not going to*
> *cut it off are you?' trembled the man. 'No. You are,'*
> *replied the husband. 'I am going to burn down the*
> *tool-shed.'*

The joke went down well. So did the rest of the paper. A few days later I was awarded the prize for the best paper of the meeting.

AFL Experiences

I have been an avid follower of the AFL team, St Kilda, for 50 years. Although much of my childhood was spent in Western Australia, everybody had to follow a Victorian team, because they were the best. I wasn't sure which one to follow until one of my mates wore a St Kilda jumper to a junior footy match in which I was playing. Not long thereafter, I went to the Subiaco oval to watch WA play Victoria. Even though WA created a major upset by winning, I was mesmerised by the big, blonde bombshell Carl Ditterich, who seemed invincible. He played for St Kilda, so that was the team for me. The fact that St Kilda had never won a premiership was not a consideration. In 1966, as an 11-year-old, I slept outside the Subiaco Oval on the Friday night so I could be in the front row to watch the WA Grand Final between Perth and East Perth. As this game got underway, the Grand Final in Victoria between Collingwood and St Kilda was drawing to a close. We were following the results on the scoreboard and I was delighted when the final score was posted showing St Kilda had won by one solitary point. I was off to a good start and thought that St Kilda would enjoy many more premierships. I am still waiting for the next one!

Nevertheless, my love for the club has not diminished. When I commenced practice, one of my surgical assistants was a good friend of the St Kilda club doctor. I made it clear that I would be happy to treat the players as required and began to be referred players for various injuries and ailments. Gradually, I came to have a more hands on role. Because I was present at most games, it was easy for me to suture any lacerations after the game and be available to advise on hand injuries. I then began to travel interstate with the team and got to know a few of the players.

In the early years, my position with the club was unofficial, so in 1997 when St Kilda were to play Adelaide in the Grand Final, my dad, brother and I lined up at the MCG around 2am, using our Melbourne Cricket Club (MCC) memberships to get the best seats in the house. My name had been placed on the MCC membership when I was 15 and I received full membership about 25 years later. It was one of my most prized possessions.

At half-time of the Grand Final, St Kilda was in front. I was able to walk from the MCC members stand, across the MCG to the St Kilda rooms. Our players were fit and seemed quietly confident. In the second half, Darren Jarman was unstoppable and Adelaide kicked 14 goals to six, taking out the game by 31 points. It was gut wrenching to watch and be a part of. After the match, standing on the MCG watching the Adelaide celebrations and in the rooms afterwards, the players were inconsolable.

Ironically, the following day we left for a family holiday... in Adelaide! As we drove along the Western Highway there were dozens of Adelaide Crows fans with their scarves hanging out the car windows driving the same way. I had to laugh however, when passing under one of the pedestrian bridges in Bacchus Marsh, someone had draped a huge sign saying, 'F***-off Crows!' It was exactly how I felt.

A few years later, when Tim Watson was coach of St Kilda, we were playing Brisbane at the Gabba. As was often the case, we were being thrashed. Towards the end of the game, I was standing with the Saints support staff just inside the boundary line. The Brisbane support staff were in a similar position about 50 metres away, when I noticed one of their trainers collapsed to the ground. The St Kilda club doctor, Ian Stone and I rushed over to find Brisbane's number one trainer was not breathing and had no pulse. He had suffered a cardiac arrest.

Having been faced with this a few times before, I got to work on his chest with cardiac compression while Ian performed mouth-to-mouth. Whilst this was occurring, the siren sounded to end the game. We were situated right in front of the Brisbane race, which dramatically tempered the celebrations of the winning Brisbane Lions team as they filed off the ground. To see their favoured head trainer, Murray Johnson, prostrate on the ground in an emergency situation was distressing for many. Not long after the Brisbane players left the field, one member of the team, Shaun Hart, returned to pray at Murray's side. We could certainly use all the help we could get. Murray was blue and things were looking grim. It seemed to take ages for the paramedics to arrive and fortunately they brought a defibrillator with them. The paddles were applied and after two shocks, Murray, regained a pulse and started breathing again. This still astonishes me. Murray's heart had stopped and he was clinically dead, yet we had been able to maintain his heart beat and oxygen supply to his vital organs, so that when his heart was restarted, his body took over.

Murray was taken to hospital and he had coronary bypass surgery the following week. He made a full recovery and subsequently returned to running for the Brisbane Lions. When the return match was played at Waverley Park, again won by Brisbane, Shaun Hart invited Ian and I into the Brisbane rooms to thank us for what we had done. Thereafter, there was a unique bond between the two clubs. Murray would always acknowledge us before every match and it was quite an amazing experience to watch him run around, doing what he loved, all because we had been taught some simple first aid as medical students. Murray passed away 13 years later and was sadly missed by the club and his family.

In 2001, Grant Thomas was appointed as coach of St Kilda Football Club. Grant was aware of some of the work that I had been doing and wanted me to have a more formal role. He felt that to have a plastic surgeon on hand at every game, to manage the cuts that players would inevitably receive, was a commitment to excellence that he wanted to pervade the club. It wasn't a difficult decision to accept for I loved adding value to a club I had supported since I was a child. Being in the rooms before a game was an eye opening experience. Over the course of two hours, seemingly ordinary young men, transformed themselves into warriors who were prepared to go to war for their mates and their team. After the game, win or lose, they began to recover their bruised and battered bodies, so they could do the same the following week.

It was not uncommon for club doctors, thinking it saved time, to suture a cut on the face or elsewhere without local anaesthetic. Although the adrenaline of the players was pretty high when they came off, they still hated this because it hurt. I put together my doctor's bag, with local anaesthetic, gauze, bandages, sutures, staples and surgical instruments. When a player came off for the blood rule, I would take them behind the race, inject local anaesthetic, suture the cut, put a small dressing on, then have them back on the field within a few minutes. The players appreciated it because it didn't hurt and their resulting scars were the best possible. If the laceration was too big, we would bandage them up and I would repair it after the game. There are still some current day players with great scars because they were looked after in this manner.

In my interaction with players, I always found them to be respectful and grateful. Many of them are decent men, whom I admired on and off the field. My daughter Rebekah, had a tiny crush on one of St Kilda's star players, Lenny Hayes. On her thirteenth birthday, I had arranged with Lenny to wish her happy birthday. I called him and when he was on the phone, told Bek there was someone on the phone who wanted to talk with her.

'Hello,' she said.

'Hi Bek. Happy birthday', said the voice on the phone.

'Thank-you. Who is this?' asked a somewhat nervous Rebekah.

'It's Lenny Hayes. I heard it was your birthday and just wanted to make sure you had a good one.'

'Oh my God! Oh my God!' said Bek, trying to compose herself and be very cool.

Bek loved it of course.

When Bek and Tim, would come into the rooms after the game, some of the players would recognise and acknowledge them. Aaron Hamill was always a big hit because he would bring some of the players' lollies over to them.

Some players understand how simple things like this can create lifelong memories for their fans. Some don't and it is their loss.

Sometimes simple gestures can create
lifelong memories for others.

On the Homefront

Rebekah was a tiny baby and for the first 18 months of her life it was easy to hold her in one hand and lift her above my head. Both she and I loved to do this. As she grew, her small size became an advantage for her in various sports. She learned to swim before she was 12 months old and developed into a very good swimmer. However, her great love was gymnastics…and she was very, very good. She had commenced gymnastics at a local club, more for fun, then took up gymnastics at school, where she was coached by a member of an advanced gymnastics club. One day the club asked to see Fiona and I, to say they had identified Rebekah as having considerable talent, which they felt could be developed to an elite level. This would require a commitment of up to 30 hours a week of gymnastics training—before and after school and at weekends—so they wanted to check us out first and get our agreement to change squads. Fiona and I discussed it with Bek and we decided that we would give her every opportunity to reach the highest level she could attain, as long as she loved it. If she didn't, she could stop at any time. Meanwhile she had our full support.

Bek's normal routine was gymnastic training on weekdays for two hours before school, two hours after school and four hours on a Saturday morning. She maintained this whilst still doing well at school. Her routine became our routine and most of the transport was provided by Fiona while I was either operating or consulting. Bek was proud of her progress, though when she would tell me about some of her training—such as climbing up a rope from floor to the roof, only using her hands, or doing the splits between raised platforms with the instructors leaning on her shoulders—I would wince and silently question whether we were doing the right thing. Nevertheless, she loved the training and particularly loved working with her coach and team of equally committed young women. At times, their courage and tenacity was breathtaking.

I found watching my child compete to be a strange experience. I was nervous, excited, satisfied, saddened, thrilled, exhilarated, sometimes within a period of a few minutes. I loved watching Bek on floor, bars and vault, her favourite apparatus, however, I hated the beam. It is such a simple piece of equipment, but it is solid, immovable and unyielding. It seemed to me that this is where she could injure herself seriously and I was always on the edge of my seat when she performed on beam.

In spite of her father's hesitation, she progressed well to the Victorian championships and then to nationals. She was identified by the national Olympics coach and was on track for higher levels. Then the injuries started.

First it was her elbow, then she broke her wrist, then injured her foot on the beam, then tore the cartilage on her hip.

It is embarrassing to acknowledge that when Bek injured her foot, she showed me when I got home. It was already bruised and painful to move—which in itself was unusual for Bek was very stoic when it came to injuries—however, in true, all-conquering doctor fashion, I said, 'She'll be right Bek, just limp.' Thankfully Fiona thought some further investigation was worthwhile and a subsequent X-ray showed Bek had fractured four of the five metatarsals. So much for my diagnostic skills!

While Bek was the social animal, Tim preferred his own space and was quite happy spending time alone. He was also taught to swim before he was 12 months old and he was at home in the pool. Fiona and I swam in squads in the early morning and from an early age Tim joined us. He developed quickly, had a beautiful stroke and had a natural affinity with butterfly, which definitely did not come from my DNA. We decided to enter him in one of the local competitions. These were full of competitors from local clubs, who took their swimming seriously. In the event schedule, Tim was described as 'unattached' and when he stood on the blocks, he seemed tiny compared with the boys around him. Nevertheless, he made the actions of a true pro warming up and when the gun went for his first heat, he shot off the blocks. He amazed us by winning his first event, 100m breaststroke by about ten body lengths. When he swam the final a little later, he bettered his heat time, but was rained in by a couple of larger boys and touched out for third. During the victory ceremony he was awarded his first medal. The fact he had managed a third, with the winners being almost twice his height, meant that he had real talent and it was clear he would benefit from more specialised training. This was confirmed when Tim told us after the meet, that someone had approached him to come and train with his club. Instead we arranged for him to attend the Melbourne Vicentre under head swimming coach Ian Pope.

It goes without saying that our family loved sport. I am frequently inspired by athletes who overcome seemingly insurmountable obstacles, to compete and even triumph. Sometimes I am thrilled by the excellence demonstrated by individuals or teams and sometimes I just love the competition, with the elation of the winners and the sorrow of the losers. It is like a microcosm of life.

Money, Money, Money

Soon after I commenced my career, I started to make some money. I knew that as time went on, my capacity to generate a considerable income would increase and my aim was to be a responsible steward of my wealth. As a profession, doctors are often not good at managing their money. We have little understanding of financial matters, are so focused on our patients and tend to be so busy, that we give our trust to others to manage our money on our behalf.

For instance, my first accountant was a family friend. I trusted his advice and he set up my structure, we incorporated a couple of companies and we embarked on what I assumed would be a lifelong partnership. A couple of years down the track I became aware that the way my finances had been set up, was on the edge of legality. I called my accountant to ask his opinion and for the first time he told me that this was a 'grey area'. Mmm! I was in agreement with some professional creativity but 'grey areas' was not part of the brief. I wanted straight up and down.

I subsequently shifted accountants, to a mid-tier firm and when they reworked my finances, we had to sell our first home in order to get up to date with the tax department. I was with this next accounting firm for a couple of years when they suggested I invest in an infrastructure project that would make money and as an added benefit, reduce my tax. Based on this advice, I invested and, some months later, my accountant informed me that the principle of this project had been found murdered in a foreign hotel room. The project was a scam.

Further to this, my only foray into the share market, was on the recommendation of a family friend, whom I thought was wealthy. I lost the entire investment as the company went into liquidation.

Many doctors are poor financial managers and are easily taken advantage of by those giving financial advice.

These were my first experiences with personal financial management. Thankfully it was still early in my career, however, it was abundantly clear that I needed a different strategy. I wanted to become personally responsible for my finances. If I had a better understanding of finance, I could make more informed decisions. I began to read books on investing and even signed up for and completed a home study course on shares, how they work and how to invest.

All-In From the Get-Go

Scarborough Beach in Western Australia is a picturesque stretch of white sandy beach not far from the centre of Perth. As a child, City Beach was my favourite, followed closely by Scarborough. When I could convince my dad, we would join a few of his mates and go for a 6am body surf in the beautiful clear waters. I loved doing something special with Dad, while catching a few waves that would pick us up out from shore and drop us close to the beach. In the late 1990s, we went on a family holiday to Scarborough Beach and I shared some of my childhood memories with my own children. After a week, the family went home while I stayed on to attend the football with St Kilda playing West Coast Eagles at Subiaco. It was a night game and as I had a few hours to spare, I passed the time in a bookshop close to the ground. I purchased a book named *Rich Dad Poor Dad*, by Robert Kiyosaki, which talked about becoming financially literate and developing financial assets that generated a cash flow. I couldn't put it down. After the game, which we won, I couldn't wait to read it on the midnight flight back to Melbourne. It was one of those *Road Less Travelled* moments that was a defining point in my life. It took me in a direction that if I had known the outcome, I might never have commenced, however, it is a direction that has made all the difference.

If I head in a particular direction, I am pretty much all in from the get go. I purchased some of Kiyosaki's tapes, then signed up for a seminar he was running in Sydney the following year. Meanwhile, I commenced playing his board game, Cashflow 101, which rewarded contestants for turning 'small deals' into 'big deals'. The winners of the game are those who can increase their passive income (money generated from investments) to be greater than their expenses. At that point they can 'retire' and live happily ever after!

In *Rich Dad Poor Dad*, Kiyosaki mentions a colleague of his who was able to buy and sell property and always make money irrespective of the market. His name was John Burley and just by chance, he was doing a seminar in Melbourne the following year. I attended and learned how to 'wrap' properties, whereby the purchaser buys an undervalued house, marks up the price and on sells it to those who are unable to get bank finance. Essentially, the original purchaser takes the risk and finances the new purchaser's acquisition. Of course, to learn how to do this properly, one is encouraged to attend a boot camp in Phoenix, Arizona, where all the secrets are revealed. This, Fiona and I did, and returned with a whole lot of information of how to do it. Information without action is useless.

Information alone is just words. Only
action, based on the information,
transforms the words into reality.

Burley had emphasised two points: Firstly, most lawyers will tell you this can't be done. He said to keep asking until you find a lawyer who knows it is legal and can be done. I called several lawyers and was told various stories why it couldn't be done. One day I called a respected friend and lawyer, who said, 'Sure, we can do that. Let me know when you would like to proceed.' That taught me a lesson. So much of the law and finance, which I had assumed was black and white, is a matter of opinion. So much of what we take as advice from professionals such as lawyers, accountants and even doctors, is opinion rather than fact. Within the same profession, there can be many differing opinions based on the same set of facts.

When seeking advice from professionals,
it is our responsibility to differentiate fact
from opinion.

Burley's second point was that most real estate agents will tell you this can't be done. Up until I set foot in the first agent's office, I could have kept things quiet. I could have gained a great deal of information that would probably be worthless in the future, however, nobody would know. Physically going into an agent's office and asking to view undervalued properties was the action that put me over the edge.

I chose a suburb in the south-east of Melbourne and a street that had a number of agent's offices in the same street. The first agent I visited said he had nothing available. It was the same story with the second agent. They both must have thought I was weird for my experience with agents is that if they don't have anything available they will take my details and call as soon as something comes up. I am still waiting for their calls.

The third agent was young and keen. He listened to my story, thought for a while and then said he might just have what I was looking for. We went for a drive into suburbia and pulled into a driveway of a decent house surrounded by other decent houses. Inside was clean and unremarkable. It even had brand new carpet in the living room. The agent told me this house was for sale for around ten per cent lower than other houses in the area. When I pushed him I discovered the house had been on the market for some time. Something wasn't adding up. It took a few more questions to discover the full story. The previous owner had been murdered in the living room. Hence, the new carpet and hence the reason why locals weren't interested in buying it. Now it all made sense!

I saw this as an opportunity for it was unlikely my prospective clients would be concerned. We purchased the house, increased the price, advertised the property for five per cent deposit with vendor finance and sold it within a few weeks, to an extremely happy purchaser. He subsequently found out about the unfortunate event that had previously taken place, however, was unconcerned because he was now living in his own home.

We had done it. We had learned some sophisticated information, taken action and completed a transaction that was a win for the original owners of the property, a win for the new owner and a win for us. Over the next few years we purchased a further dozen under-valued properties (mostly those that required some renovation work) and on-sold them to very grateful buyers. For the next ten years, property prices continued to rise, so the new purchasers developed equity in their properties. All subsequently attained bank finance, paid out their debt to us, and continued living in their own homes. This was one of our investment success stories.

Investment in shares is another story. There is an attraction to shares in that it feels like you have more control (you can buy and sell at any time) and there is a potential for a greater return in a shorter period of time. I attended several share investment courses, read books and even learned to chart shares. I learned to buy and hold, then trade shares on a weekly and even daily basis. I learned to set in place so called fail safe, stop losses, which was an indication to sell if the price dropped below the set figure. My first trade resulted in a more than 100 per cent return in a few days. It is possibly the worst thing that could have happened because from then on I thought I was an invincible genius of share market trading. Unfortunately, that was far from the case and when the dot com crash occurred, it mattered little how many stop losses were in place. I went down with it.

A Life Well Lived

Around this time, my mum and dad, Colonel and Mrs Frank Linsell, retired from active service in the Salvation Army. Dad could have retired at 65 but elected to do another year. His role at the time was Chief Secretary of the Australian Southern Territory, which meant he was second in charge of the Salvation Army's work in Southern Australia. In character, Dad was not unlike his own father. He was charismatic, creative, funny, warm and seemingly liked by all, except for those under his command, who had taken advantage of the trust afforded them in their roles as Salvation Army officers. Dad was intensely fair, however, he had the courage to hold people to account when they broke the rules.

For a Salvation Army Officer, he held a broad view of the world, being the first officer to attend the Mt Eliza Business School, to develop his leadership, and along with Mum, they were among the early attendees at the Officer's Training College for officers in London. Mum and Dad held leadership positions in Singapore/Malaysia and the USA, before returning to Australia to finish their careers as Chief Secretaries. Dad was intensely loyal to his God, his Church, to his superiors and to his mission of spreading the gospel of Jesus Christ.

I found Dad to be at his best when he was heading the public relations department of the Salvation Army. He loved being creative, meeting new people and working for the Army. He and his co-workers in the department were very productive and along the way became fast friends, while having a lot of fun. Dad set up the advisory board by attracting successful business people to give of their time on a board that advised the Army leadership how to respond to current events and how to plan for the future. He also had a good deal to do with the launching of the Red Shield Appeal. Until that time there had been a mismatch of smaller appeals for funds, however, the Red Shield Appeal centralised the administration and it became a national appeal, universally recognised and supported by all Australians.

Dad loved his food and the closest he came to exercise was when he reached for the remote control to change television stations. His favourite show was *Fawlty Towers*. He had watched the series so many times, he knew the dialogue by heart. With a poor diet and lack of exercise for most of the latter half of his life, he was overweight. It is not surprising he developed Type-2 diabetes, eventually requiring insulin injections to keep his blood sugar level stable.

When Dad retired, to me, he seemed lost. He had devoted his life to helping others and with the Salvation Army's military structure, was used to taking orders. Every week, he would spend a couple of days at the Juvenile Court, doing what he could to help other Salvation Army officers with their roles. In times like this, his humility shone through and I suspect it was a conscious choice to work in the courts, given this is where his father had the most impact. Every Wednesday, Dad would drive me to my rooms in country Victoria. I had developed a practice in Gippsland, had purchased rooms and visited on a weekly basis. Dad offered to drive me there (about two hours), wait in the kitchen while I consulted, then drive me the two hours back. I loved these times. That Dad was so generous with his time and presence is something I will always remember. However, he rarely shared anything of himself. I wanted to know about him, about his early life, what he was thinking and feeling. As seems to be true for many men of his era, he was uncomfortable talking about himself and was content to drive in silence. His actions demonstrated how proud he was of me, yet I never recall him saying so. Then again, if I had to choose between words and actions, I will take actions every time.

In Dad's 69th year, he noticed a lump in his neck. After a surgical biopsy he was diagnosed with non-Hodgkin lymphoma. He was treated with chemotherapy, which he undertook with great grace and became cancer free. He celebrated his 70th birthday at our house surrounded by his friends and family, telling the same jokes and laughing at the same stories as they had done for years. A few months later, the lymphoma recurred around the same time that he had a heart attack. My dad was dying and he knew it. There was no panic and he expressed no regrets. It struck me how graceful and dignified he remained.

Just after his 71st birthday, the family gathered at his bedside in hospital. The end was not far off and Dad was lapsing in an out of consciousness. I asked to spend some time with him alone. He was unconscious as I said my goodbyes, expressing some of the things I hadn't understood about our relationship, yet telling him how much I loved him and would miss him.

I had to leave the hospital. I had operated that day and one of my own patients had a haematoma and required a further operation. I drove to my own hospital, with tears streaming down my face, knowing I had just seen Dad for the last time. I arrived at the operating theatre and there was a phone call waiting for me. Derek told me Dad had just passed away. I went from that phone call into the operating theatre, to operate on my own patient. It is one of the hardest things I have ever had to do.

The funeral service was for family only, held at the Springvale crematorium. Dad's Salvation Army cap adorned his casket and the words of Celine Dion singing 'My Heart Will Go On' was piped through. I am not sure I liked the song before and I definitely don't now, for every time I hear it, it anchors me back to Dad's casket!

His memorial service was held immediately afterwards and as I drove to it, I remember taking a call from a patient and I reassured them all was okay following their operation. Dad's memorial service was a celebration of a fulfilled life of service to God and others. I'd attended quite a few funerals before, however, this was the first time I had sat in the front row. It was a strange time of supporting my children with their grief, being grateful to those who had attended and at the same time dealing with my own grief. Countless people came up to me to tell me how my dad had touched their lives. Several of his friends and co-workers also told me how, unbeknown to me, he would tell them how proud he was of me. I wish he had told me himself whilst he was alive.

Note to parents: If you love your children
and are proud of them, tell them.

My father left me a wonderful legacy. He was a man of patience, kindness, humility, creativity, strength, courage, fun and laughter. He could laugh at himself and he could laugh with others. I could not have asked for more. I am very blessed.

Not long after Dad died, I attended a plastic surgery conference in New York. It was at this meeting, I first heard the term 'anti aging' and learned that there were things that could be done to prevent disease and prolong life.

Already, I was very fit, swimming in a squad five mornings a week and very disciplined with my eating. I would soon swim at the World Masters Games to be held in Melbourne and placed in the top 20 for my age group. Having watched my dad die way too young, I felt I had a message regarding optimal health to share with any who would listen. One of the ways to do this was to run my own health seminar.

I enlisted the help of a Dr Brett Forge (the cardiologist who had correctly admonished me some ten years earlier) as well as my brother Derek, a first class and powerful communicator. The seminar, held in July 2001, was entitled 'Add More Days to your Life And More Life to your Days' and focused on having a healthy balance in life. It was about making conscious choices in life that gave us the greatest possibility of living a long and fruitful life. During my presentation, I shared that no-one wants to live longer if they are simply existing. Life is so much more than existence. A long life that is still fun, enjoyable and fulfilling is something to which most people aspire. The 30 attendees, a mixture of patients and friends, were appreciative of the quality of the information and felt they received good value. Furthermore, I enjoyed the teaching and presenting from the front of the room.

To Be the Best Person I Could Be

When I had become a plastic surgeon, one of the first books I read was Stephen Covey's classic, *The Seven Habits of Highly Effective People*. This book had a profound impact on me for it focused on a person's character. Effectiveness in life stems from having true values in place and living according to principles aligned with these values. I was particularly struck with the exercise he suggested whereby you picture yourself at a funeral, with the eulogies about to start and then realise it is your own funeral. Covey urges the reader to consider, what is it that you would like people to be saying about you. As I considered this, I wanted to inspire people, to make a difference and to be the best person I could possibly be.

Over the next ten years, one of my favourite things to do was while away some time in a bookshop. Invariably, I would find my way to the self-help section, which is why I came to be reading the book by Anthony Robbins, *Awaken the Giant Within*. Until then, I had attended a few investment seminars but had resisted attending so called personal development seminars. However, Tony Robbins was coming to Melbourne and I thought I might learn something whilst having some fun.

I attended an 'Unleash the Power Within' seminar in Melbourne in late 1991. I was sceptical to start with but was soon won over with the production, the music, the content and Robbins' dynamism. I knew a fire walk was involved but I had no idea this would take place on the first night. In spite of the preparation he had taken us through, I had considerable trepidation and not an inconsequential amount of fear. The coals were darn hot. I recall considering the very real possibility that I would end up in the emergency department of my own teaching hospital, only a stone's throw away, where I knew the head of the Burns Unit. I could imagine her saying, 'Now you are here because you were doing...*what?*'

In spite of this, I walked across ten metres of hot coals, silently chanting, 'Cool moss, cool moss,' and was amazed that when I got to the end, I was not suffering from full thickness burns to the soles of my feet. I had a lot of fun over the next few days and when I came home, I told Fiona that I had signed up for another bunch of programs. Fiona had been unable to attend this event because she had taken Bek to a gymnastics competition. Fiona surprised me by saying she would like to accompany me on the next event, 'Date with Destiny', to be held on the Gold Coast early the following year. During this event we were introduced to the possibility of becoming Platinum Partners, which was a select number of people from around the world, who would meet for four events, led by Tony, over a 12-month period. Fiona and I discussed it and decided this is what we would like to do. Within a few months, we became two more of Tony Robbins' Platinum Partners.

The first event was held at Skibo Castle in Scotland. With these events, there was no expense spared with helicopters, limousine transfers, suites, dinners etc. Tony ensured that these would be experiences to remember and that the friendships forged would be long-term.

Skibo was once the home of Andrew Carnegie, who was once the wealthiest person in the world. To listen to lectures about finance in the former home of the world's wealthiest man gives the lectures a special edge. At this event, we met a fellow Australian who ran his own seminars on wealth creation. I explained about my poor experiences with share trading and he told me he had developed a system for trading shares, which was consistently realising above average returns. I became friends with Paul and looked forward to him teaching us his system upon our return to Australia.

Subsequent Platinum Partner trips were to Vancouver, which included travelling by seaplane to Whistler in the summer, then to Morocco, which included a private-jet charter to the edge of the

Sahara Desert. We were to stay in tents, which initially didn't thrill me, however, when the transport was via camel and dune buggy, and the tents were air-conditioned, five-star luxury, I was a little more amenable. The following morning, I was up early to watch the magnificence of the sunrise. The quietness of the dawn was temporarily broken by another dune buggy roaring up to my vantage point. It was Tony Robbins and we shared a few minutes watching the sunrise from the edge of the Sahara Desert. I had dinner with Tony a few times and found him to be charming, engaging and charismatic. What I didn't like was that all attendees had to abide by what was known as Tony time. This meant that all had to wait for Tony, who was sometimes one or even two hours late for a specific appointment. This, to me, was disrespectful of other people's time indicating he felt his time was more important than ours.

Keeping a time commitment is respectful
of all parties involved.

Our final dinner on the Moroccan trip, was held in a massive tent, taking the form of an Arabian bazaar, complete with snake charmers, carpet sellers, spices, an abundance of food and dancing. These magnificent experiences were put together by one of Tony's staff, Jan Cabe Avant, and they remain the best event experiences I have attended.

The final event of the Platinum year was to be held at Tony's Fijian resort, Namale. A few weeks out from the event, Fiji was hit by a cyclone. A week from the event, Tony cancelled, presumably because of the cyclone, however, it was felt by more than a few that he had a more pressing engagement closer to the USA and the cyclone became a justification rather than a reason for cancelling. A few of us had already booked our flights and time off, so we decided to go to Fiji and find alternative accommodation. We selected a place called Lomalagi, which means 'Heaven', so it sounded exotic and romantic. Whilst the location was spectacular, if Heaven means suffering through communal dinners, where the quantity of food is under strict control, I think it will be more fun in the other place!

Whilst we were there, we heard about a group who were doing some sort of retreat. They kept to themselves and only ordered room service. This in itself seemed to be a very smart idea. A few days later I walked into the reception area of the resort to find two people whom I had not seen before. I introduced myself to Bill and Betty (not their real names) and they said they had been leading a private retreat. They seemed well fed so clearly they had done better with room service than we had done with communal eating. They were travelling the world and occasionally had people fly into a resort where they would spend some time working through their issues. They had worked in the seminar and personal development industry for several years and dropped a few names such as Robert Kiyosaki and Tony Robbins. They intrigued me and when Bill left his business card with the resort owner to ask me to call him, I decided to check them out further when we returned to Melbourne.

A Bedrock Founded on Sand

At this stage, my plastic surgical practice was called 'New You Lifestyle Centres'. My vision was to make a difference in people's lives primarily through cosmetic surgery, whilst providing products and services that catered for people's physical, mental, emotional and spiritual needs. My longer-term plan was to establish several New You Lifestyle Centres throughout Australia and, if successful, internationally.

As the cosmetic surgical side of my practice was expanding and was more lucrative, I had made a decision to cease doing skin cancer work and refer all of these patients to one of my colleagues. This is another of my greatest regrets. I did not appreciate it at the time, but with this decision I lost a bit of my soul. My skin cancer patients were salt of the earth people who always kept me grounded. I had developed long-term relationships with many of them and did not appreciate how valuable this was to me. It was a business decision to focus on what I thought was more lucrative. I now see this as a mistake. As a doctor, my practice is first and foremost a profession as well as being a business. Yes, it must make money, however, patients are not like widgets, where you can bypass some because another type makes more money.

*Not all business decisions should focus on
the bottom line.*

When we returned to Melbourne, I researched Bill and Betty's website. I was staggered to find their plan was to establish multiple lifestyle centres around the world, each of which catered for an individual's physical, mental, emotional and spiritual needs. It was almost identical to my personal vision but on a larger scale. I wanted to learn more about them.

My friend Paul and I flew to Sydney to spend a day with them and not long after, Fiona and I took Bek and Tim to Noosa, where we spent some more time with them. They appeared to be genuine people. They had both had corporate careers before independently entering the seminar business, she as a presenter and he as a producer. They felt that the personal development industry had too many people taking advantage of others and wanted to change that by setting up a company that was highly ethical from the top down.

This, of course, was aligned with my own thoughts and they seemed to be speaking my language.

We all felt that the next step was to attend one of their events. This was not undertaken lightly for we had just finished the Platinum Partner year—somewhat dissatisfied—and we were less than enthusiastic about spending further money and time on events. Nevertheless, Paul and his partner, Fiona and I registered for their Platinum Partner equivalent and attended an event in Phuket. This turned out to be better than I had expected. The content was fresh and because the attendee numbers were small, Bill and Betty spent time with each of us, particularly helping us to crystallise what we would like to be doing in the future. The attendees were a mixture of people from Singapore, New Zealand and Australia and all seemed to be decent human beings who wanted to make a difference in other people's lives, whilst being the best people they could be. Most of it was fun. I was introduced to yoga for the first time and we were placed in groups for team building exercises and games. In the team games, my competitiveness surprised me. I wanted to win and played full out in order to do so.

It was at this event that they began to talk about business. Their model for establishing lifestyle centres around the world was to sell licences for geographical regions. They suggested that we four Australians would be ideal candidates to purchase the rights to establish centres in Australia. The cost was US$500,000. At the time the Australian dollar was hovering around US65c so the true cost to us would be more like A$750,000. They put it to us that it was only US$125,000 each. In anybody's language it is still a lot of money for a licence!

Upon our return to Australia, Paul's partner had some misgivings. I wish I had listened more, however, I wanted Bill and Betty to be real. I was enamoured with the bigger picture, with the vision and at the time, the details of the plan were not that important. Big mistake and very costly!

In business, the vision is important,
however, even more crucial is a detailed
and plausible plan to implement
the vision.

We attended another event about six months later, this time in Hawaii. Again the content was fresh, exciting and seemed to be original. Again the vision of being the world's greatest lifestyle company was shared and this was a vision with which I was aligned. I wanted to be involved. Just how I wasn't sure. Short-term gain wasn't of interest to me. I wanted to invest in the parent company. Whilst the returns would take longer, they would eventually be greater. It meant we would have more control and we would not be working in the business on a full-time basis.

Attending events, listening to content, learning and applying what is relevant is one thing. Doing business with the people leading the events is a totally different ballgame. Unfortunately, I didn't make the distinction and I was totally unprepared for negotiations about investment and the business. We did not do our due diligence. We did not ask the right questions of the people involved or their previous business acquaintances, or explore their previous success or otherwise, or dissect the business plan in detail. We did not seek advice from family, trusted friends, colleagues, business people, lawyers or finance experts. If we had, we almost certainly would not have moved ahead for there was a lot of rhetoric but the detail was flimsy. What we were missing was wise independent advice.

If you are planning to do business with
or invest in others, do your due diligence
and know the right questions to ask.

The question I have asked myself many times since then is why did I move forward with the purchase of a licence agreement without seeking independent advice. The answer is because I wanted it to happen. I was aligned with and enrolled in the vision and the bigger picture. The finer details, I felt, were unimportant. I was prepared to deal with the consequences. The willingness to take a risk for something I believe in is a character trait some might consider reckless. Certainly, this decision, in time, tested every fibre of my being. I have become the person I am today, because of the choices I made at that time. If I had my time again, would I make different choices? Absolutely! Making mistakes is part of being human. Learning from them and doing things differently in the future entails the gaining of wisdom.

The Road Less Travelled is not for the faint
hearted, it might test all that you are…
and this is what makes all the difference.

Putting a Price on My Life's Work

Throughout this time, as well as working in my practice, I had been working on my practice. My aim was to implement systems into the business that would provide a seamless experience for our patients. And I wanted the patient experience to be exceptional. As the vast majority of my patients were women seeking cosmetic surgery, I sought to understand more of what women wanted. I asked a group of previous patients to give me advice on how they thought the experience could be improved. For most women, the choice for cosmetic surgery does not come lightly. It is often a one-off decision, which is often accompanied by a great deal of fear and guilt. I also knew the outcomes made an enormous difference to the women concerned, which made it all worthwhile. I wanted to make the experience more than an operation and something that was memorable and enjoyable.

We introduced limousine transfers to and from the hospital. We knew that day three after an operation was often the lowest point. This is when the initial adrenaline and excitement of coming through the procedure is replaced by pain and doubt, particularly if the patient has gone home to a house where she is still expected to be super mum. We would send flowers on day three along with a follow up phone call just to make sure all was well. Further to that we would arrange for a cleaner to attend during the first week, to clean her house so she could rest rather than doing the things she would normally be doing. For ladies who had facelifts, we would arrange for their hair to be done during the first couple of weeks. During post op visits, we would give out vouchers for new bras along with Gold Class cinema tickets. We wanted our patients to experience something special with every visit to our clinic. We wanted them to know they were respected, amongst friends and that they were supported every step of the way. Most surgeons are skilled at what they do. The operative outcomes of each procedure are not that different from one surgeon to another. However, not every practice provides these special additional touches and it was often these things that women talked about with other women, helping to enrich the reputation of the practice.

One of the issues for many doctors in solo practice is that at the end of their careers, they are unable to sell their business. In business terms, they have built up lots of 'good will', however, selling this to another doctor is quite uncommon. Many young doctors think that there is no need to purchase an existing practice when they can set up next door and wait for the incumbent to retire. This is one of the reasons why becoming part of a larger group has become more popular. The group might pay the doctor a fee to purchase the practice then pay an ongoing service fee whilst the doctor continues to work in the practice. This is now commonplace for general practitioners. In 2004, it was extremely uncommon for surgeons.

With another of those 'Road Less Travelled' decisions, I decided to sell my practice. At that time, I had not decided to leave plastic surgery, however, it would give me more flexibility, if this is what I decided to do. Having said that, I knew of no other Australian plastic surgeon who had sold their practice. Those I did know who had retired, had simply walked away. Nevertheless, I made it known throughout the plastic surgical circles in Australia and New Zealand, as well as making calls to those I thought might be interested. Nobody was. It was several months before I received a single call from a plastic surgeon on the Gold Coast. He had just sold his practice to a business entity that was interested in purchasing plastic surgical practices.

'Could the CEO of the business give you a call?' he said.

'Sure can,' I answered. I was very excited.

Sure enough, the CEO gave me a call shortly thereafter. They were indeed looking to purchase plastic surgical practices, run the administration of the practices and pay surgeons a service fee to work in the practice. This could be the original surgeon in the practice, but that was not essential as the plan was to employ multiple surgeons to work in different locations. If they could make it work, it was a great plan and I was very interested.

Negotiating the value of a plastic surgical practice was not an easy matter as few precedents had been set previously. Nevertheless, the alternative for me was to walk away with nothing, so the prospect of receiving some funds was exciting. As negotiations took place, the proposal was for me to receive an upfront payment with the balance paid off over a four-year period. Furthermore, I would be given a 12-month contract to continue to work in my practice, while they engaged other surgeons to work in my place. When my lawyer reviewed the contract for the sale of the practice, he contacted me to ask whether I wanted to include a clause that in the event of default on payment, the transaction would become null and void, with the ownership returning to me. I considered this, however, by this stage I was ready to move on and was happy to walk away. The clause was therefore omitted.

This was a mistake. If the clause had been included it would have given me options in the case of a default on payment. It has often been said, that when moving towards a dream, you should have no plan B. 'Never give up' is also a catchcry often bandied around. It is a bit like Hernán Cortés who upon travelling across the ocean from Spain to invade Mexico, ordered his troops to burn their boats. This meant there was no means of a retreat. It was win or bust, conquer or die. I had bought into this and my experience has now taught me that having a plan B and maybe a plan C or D, is a good idea. Not having a plan B, can mean that there is a reluctance to cut losses early. All good business people know when to cut their losses. When I was focused on getting into medicine, my stubbornness, resilience and refusal to give up worked in my favour. In business and particularly where money was concerned, it worked against me.

In business a plan B is a good thing.

When the deed was signed I was one of the first plastic surgeons in Australia to successfully negotiate the sale of their practice. It was a bit strange turning up for work in my own rooms, knowing that my loyal staff were now employed by another company and I was contracted to the practice. I was disappointed to learn that one of the first things they did was remove all the value adds that we had built up over time. It was a typical cost cutting business decision, however, I felt they were short sighted in doing away with the practice's 'point of difference'.

Nevertheless, as a contractor I had a lot more freedom and I was ready for the next phase of my life. However, nothing could have prepared me for what was to happen!

Part Six
The Getting of Wisdom!

Expensive Lessons

In the year 2000, Sydney hosted the Summer Olympics for the first time. Although living in Melbourne at the time, we entered the ballot for tickets and were successful for many of the events we wanted to see. Fiona, Bek, Tim and I travelled to Sydney by car. Accommodation was at a premium and we were fortunate to stay at a fabulous property in Palm Beach, generously provided by a plastic surgical colleague in Sydney. Sydney was magnificent. Its natural beauty is incomparable and its people were on their best behaviour. Everywhere we went, whether they were volunteers, paid staff or people in the street, they were friendly and fun. It was so much fun to be part of the whole experience.

The standout events were the swimming, where we saw Susie O'Neill win the 200m freestyle, and the beach volleyball. The music, the crowd participation and the excellence of the athletes made the beach volleyball an exceptional event.

We had so much fun in Sydney, we decided to attend the summer games in Athens in 2004. Tickets for premium events in Athens were a little more difficult to come by, however, we took our chances and went anyway. At the time, Tim's swimming coach at the Melbourne Vicentre was Ian Pope, with whom I had become friends. Ian had coached Matt Welsh to Silver and Bronze medals in Sydney 2000, however, although Matt was swimming in Athens along with four other swimmers from his squad, Ian was not on the Australian coaching panel. This didn't worry Ian. One of Ian's swimmers was the Italian Massimiliano Rosolino and the Italian television network covering the games asked Ian to work with them. This meant Ian had a media pass which gave him entrance into any event he desired. As Ian didn't have any accommodation organised, he stayed with us in our hotel room. We had a ball! Furthermore, with the swimming heats in the morning, if the competitors failed to make the finals, they would often give away their tickets to the evening final events. As Ian knew a lot of people in the swimming world, he would end up with premium seats to the swimming finals and I would tag along. In this way, Fiona and I were sitting next to Grant Hackett's mum and dad when Grant won the 1500m, with a partially collapsed lung.

On another night, I was privileged to witness one of the greatest races ever staged. It was the men's 200m freestyle. Billed as 'The Race of the Century', it featured four of the fastest swimmers ever to perform at the Olympics. Ian Thorpe, in his trademark full-length black suit, Pieter van den Hoogenband from the Netherlands, Michael Phelps, the rising superstar from the USA and Grant Hackett. The Dutchman was the defending Olympic champion and for the first part of the race he was under world-record time. Thorpe was trailing for the first three laps, then in the final lap, he went to another level and simply powered away. Thorpe seemed to be 'in the zone', touching out Hoogenband for second with Phelps third. It was remarkable to watch. Magnificent athletes at the top of their game, giving everything they had. It was thrilling and so inspirational.

Meanwhile, back in Australia, whilst we were having fun at the Olympics, my business partner Paul was organising the first event under the new licencing agreement. We arrived back in Australia just in time for the event presented by Bill and Betty and it was well received by the attendees. I was therefore shocked when Paul took me aside on day two to tell me he and his partner had decided to pull out of the agreement. They had already paid US$125,000 as had we, however, they felt it was not for them and did not want to follow through. He didn't say it at the time, however, I can now see they were cutting their losses. This left Fiona and I with a dilemma. Do we also pull out, breaking a contract and going back on our word, or do we move forward, complete the payment on our own and follow through with my dream to establish lifestyle centres around Australia?

A short time prior to the Australian event a group of Singaporean partners had entered into a similar licencing agreement with Bill and Betty. They had set up a Singaporean company named Bedrock Singapore (not its real name), commenced running their own events and had developed a purpose-built centre to run the company and deliver the events. When Fiona and I visited the Bedrock Singapore Centre and talked with the Singaporean partners, it was clear they were well ahead of us. It seemed to us, that the quickest way to move Australia forward would be to move to Singapore and work in the existing business. Shifting careers was one thing; shifting countries with a young family (Bek was 15, Tim was 14) was another.

We talked it through as a family and decided that we could and should do it. In April 2005, we packed our things, put some furniture and winter clothes in storage and moved countries, for what we thought would be 12 months. I continued to work as a plastic surgeon for the company that had purchased my business. Whilst

I lived in Singapore, I would travel to Australia for ten days every month to consult and operate. Because the company now owned practices on both the Gold Coast and in Melbourne, I worked in both places. This is where I learned it was possible to live in one location and work in another. I got used to a long commute while my Qantas Frequent Flyer points and Qantas status credits continued to increase.

We found a fabulous apartment to rent just off Orchard Road, the centre of Singapore's shopping district. Rent, however, was at least double what we would pay for similar space and facilities in Australia. The children were enrolled in the American school and for the first time we employed a maid. The transition seemed to have gone well save for the fact that soon after we arrived, we were asked to loan personal funds to Bedrock Singapore. Thinking this would be a one-off and wanting to show our commitment, we loaned the funds. In retrospect this was a major warning sign for what was to come.

A business that requires a loan of personal
funds for working capital should ring
alarm bells.

The business encouraged husbands and wives to work together. Two families from New Zealand joined several Singaporean based families as well as our own. Initially there was a lot of camaraderie and support for each other, however, as time went on and money got tighter, relationships were tested. Events were held in both Singapore and Bali and attendees always seemed to receive a lot of value from them. The events and their delivery were outstanding. In other words, the product was excellent. I thought it was a matter of time until the business became very profitable.

We began to work long hours in the business and spare time was unusual. One of the casualties of this was regular attendance at church. I still had and still have, a deep sense of God, however, found I was more open to other expressions of faith. There is much I don't understand in life, however, I have a strong sense that we are all spiritual beings, connected, with way more similarities than differences. I also believe that if there is a commitment to do the right thing, things tend to work out for the better.

A few months after we arrived, Bill and Betty suggested Bedrock Singapore should raise capital to assist with working capital. I had never raised capital before, however, as I was so passionate about the project, believing also that the return on investment for their shareholding would be exceptional, I shared the opportunity with a few of my friends. In a short period of time, I had personally raised SG$300,000 while the business raised a lot more.

With any capital that was raised for the business a minimum of 50 per cent (and usually a lot more) would be forwarded to Bill and Betty's company, primarily to pay for ongoing licence agreements. Over the next few years, Bedrock Singapore raised millions of dollars from investors who purchased shares, or those who took out convertible notes or simply loaned money to the company. Irrespective of how the company was doing, each time funds came in, a minimum of 50 per cent was forwarded to Bill and Betty's company. If it didn't all hell broke loose.

Bill and Betty controlled the business by controlling the people working in the business. No decision of any consequence was made without their approval. Not that they ever became directors or invested any of their personal funds in the company. They saw themselves as consultants to the Bedrock Singapore board, yet held total sway over the composition of the board and its decisions.

In spite of the issues the company faced, I believed in its mission and the people with whom I was working. Whilst money was tight in the business and salaries were often not paid, our family was reasonably well protected as I was still travelling back to Australia to consult and operate, which meant we had revenue from my surgical work as well as monthly payments from the sale of my practice. In retrospect, I would have been wise to have kept things as they were until Bedrock Singapore was more stable. However, my passion for making a difference in many people's lives was still strong. To do that I felt I needed to work full-time in the Bedrock Singapore business.

When 2006 dawned, I was full of optimism. It turned out to be one of the worst years of my life. Early in the year, I announced to the CEO of the company that had purchased my plastic surgical practice that I was no longer prepared to work as a contracted plastic surgeon. My contract had expired and I felt the timing was right for me to move out of medicine into business. The monthly payments for the sale of the practice would continue as there was nothing in the contract to say the payments were conditional on me working in the practice. However, a month or so later, I received notification that if I no longer worked in the practice, the practice company would go into liquidation and be wound up. There had never been any indication the practice company had cash flow issues so this came as a shock. If the company went into liquidation, the monthly payments would cease.

Whilst I was considering this, in the February, Fiona and I along with three other couples attended a 'Relationship Week' event in Bali, run by Bill and Betty. Three of the four couples were married with young children. The event was billed as a means to improve a couple's relationship, by getting to know each other in a deeper way. The reality was that the event was disruptive to each relationship. This wasn't obvious to ourselves at the time for we felt the rigor of the microscope we were all placed under, would be of value to us in the long-term. However, within a few years, the unmarried couple were no longer together and all three married couples were divorced.

It was during this event that I decided I would not return to plastic surgery. The monthly payments from the practice company stopped immediately, meaning they had only paid about half of the amount agreed to when I sold my practice. Not long after the company was placed in liquidation. Shortly thereafter, a new company was commenced, with the same office holders and only a slightly different name. This company retained all the assets that I had originally sold to them and for which I would receive no further payment. This so-called phoenix manoeuvre is now illegal, but in 2006, my legal advice was that the chances of winning a legal action were not high. My money was gone.

I made the decision to leave surgery during a period when I was under significant stress. This is far from optimal. Although I had been considering it for some time, making a major decision that would impact the rest of my life and my family's life, whilst under stress, was a mistake.

Never, ever make a decision with long-term consequences when under stress.

I was offered a job with one of Bill and Betty's companies. I lasted a month. Another three-day, very intense event was held at the end of that time and, as a direct result, Fiona and I separated. I was called to the office of Bedrock Singapore where Bill, Betty, Fiona and a few others informed me of the decision that had been made. I was shocked and devastated. It happened so suddenly and I felt torn apart inside as, with little preparation, I said goodbye to Bek and Tim. It did not seem right. I was desperately sad and it was one of the lowest points of my life.

Annus Horribilis

Fiona's status in Bedrock Singapore was rising. Mine was not. I was asked to leave the company. I made the decision to return to Australia and return to plastic surgery in order to regain some stability in my life and that of my family. I contacted two of my plastic surgical colleagues in Queensland to ask if they would be interested in contracting me to their practices. It was through their generosity and willingness to help, that I began working with Dr Mark Vucak in Townsville, Rockhampton and Mackay, and Dr Isolde Hertess in Cairns. I arrived in Townsville with my suitcase and began work not long afterward. I borrowed heavily on my credit cards, hired accommodation in Noosa, then Cairns and travelled between the various centres consulting and operating. If you have good back-up facilities with patient care being paramount, it is not that difficult to be a fly in, fly out surgeon. It is also facilitated by the quality of the transport between cities.

Fiona stayed in Singapore with the children and we spoke on a regular basis. I had no intention of ending the marriage and it was my sole priority to be back with Fiona and my family. Meanwhile, I learned to cook and learned to dance so when Bek and Tim came to stay during the school holidays, we had a lot of fun. My handmade chocolate mousse in particular went down very well.

Meanwhile, my mum was dying. When dad died six years previously, they had been married 46 years and in the following years she had really struggled. Mum was a strong and courageous woman, with a heart for God and a heart for her family. As a child she had to cope with poverty and a fractured family. She told us a story of having to wear her older brother's 'big, black boots' to school because she had nothing else. She was so embarrassed she stood in the corner and tried to hide one boot at a time behind her other leg. As a child I was aware finances were tight, however, because Mum was a disciplined budgeter, we always seemed to have enough food and clothes and never felt we were deprived of holidays. Mum was fiercely determined and intelligent. She wrote well and spoke well. After her retirement, Derek and I encouraged her to attend university or at least to write her story. I think she would have excelled and loved it at the same time.

Mum was diagnosed with cancer of unknown origin. Not once did I hear her complain about her condition or her treatment, even though it was quite debilitating for her. Her faith never wavered and she was confident she was going to be with Jesus and with her beloved Frank. Whilst visiting her in hospital in Melbourne, we both knew the end was coming soon. She was not afraid. She was at peace. I said goodbye to her knowing I would never see her again and then a little later by phone from Queensland. I told her how much I loved her, how much I admired her, and how grateful I was that she was my mum.

I was in the rooms in Cairns, in the middle of a minor procedure list, when I received a call to inform me Mum had passed away. I had already administered the local anaesthetic so I had to complete the procedure. As with the passing of my dad, I went straight from news of Mum's death to operating. It was again extremely difficult, however, most medical practitioners I have observed are good at compartmentalising their feelings in order to do what is best for the patient. Where we often struggle is dealing with them at a later time.

We held Mum's funeral in a similar fashion to Dad's, with a private service followed by a memorial service. As I hadn't seen Mum for a few weeks, Bill suggested I ask the undertaker to allow me to see her privately before the service, with the top off the coffin. I was grateful for the suggestion for this was easier and more rewarding than I had expected. Mum looked very peaceful and content. I said my final goodbyes and kissed her for the last time. I was very moved—and at least Celine Dione wasn't singing in the background.

I miss both my mum and dad, for they died at too young an age. They left me a rich heritage and there are times I would love to call them up and share what has been happening in my life. Would they be proud of their three children and their four grandchildren? I not only think so, I know so. For me they were perfect and if I can emulate the character traits that I so admired in them such as love, compassion, integrity, courage, resilience, passion, persistence and a heart for others, they have passed on a legacy that is priceless.

2006 had not been a great year. I had lost hundreds of thousands of dollars that was to fund my transition of career. Shortly afterwards, after 17 years of marriage, my wife and I separated. A few months later, my mother died.

Fortunately, Fiona mellowed over the course of the year and we both agreed we wanted to be together. The plan was for me to return to Singapore and the family late in the year and leave medicine forever. In December 2006, I performed my last operation, a liposuction, and never expected to lift a scalpel again. I was appointed to a position in Bedrock Singapore and left Australia once again.

From Bad To Rock Bottom

In spite of a group of passionate and committed people, over the next few years Bedrock Singapore slowly died. I spent a lot of this time working for the company in Australia and I was not seeing my family for months at a time. Money became extremely scarce. We took our children out of private school and they entered the Singaporean public school system. We continued to downgrade our accommodation and even then we struggled to pay rent. For one period of time, I was in Australia, Bek was boarding with one family and Fiona and Tim were with another. This was a major challenge for us all. I had never been short of money before, however, we had to survive. We began to sell or pawn our jewellery. Our watches went to generate cash, as did our wedding rings. I began to ask family and friends for personal loans. This was far from easy, however, there were times we had minimal cash and nothing in the bank. To those who said yes, I am eternally grateful. They probably had no idea how tough things were for us, but that they trusted in me enough to loan personal funds is something I will never forget.

This was also immensely challenging for Bek and Tim. In a reasonably short period of time, they had gone from a privileged private school education in both Australia and Singapore, to the Singapore public system, with occasional reverse racism and at times feeling hungry because there was not much to eat. Yet, in spite of the difficulties, we came through it together. Bek and Tim have demonstrated the ability to adapt to any circumstance and make the most of it, with grace and good humour. They have learned not to take anything or anyone for granted. Their resilience has been an inspiration to me. I could not be more proud of them.

With our personal struggles, we were no worse off than our colleagues in the business. Everyone was suffering and it is simply remarkable that so many of us lasted as long as we did. You may ask, as I have subsequently done many times, why did we continue to do what we were doing, with minimal return other than the thanks of grateful clients? The answer is that at the time, both Fiona and I believed that we had an outstanding product. Furthermore, we believed the plan for delivering the product and the business plan would eventually be shown to be correct. To my great regret, I was wrong. I now know the plan was flawed and the people who had created the plan were not worthy of my trust.

One of the easiest things to do is lay blame. I have found that if I blame others for an unexpected outcome, then I learn nothing and am likely to repeat the same mistake. The only way I learn and grow is by owning my mistakes, learning from them and committing to never repeat them. I am responsible for my own decisions, choices and therefore outcomes. My responsibility was to do my own due diligence on those in whom I placed my trust. It was up to me to check past business dealings, past business and personal relationships, check references and seek advice from trusted sources, before making a decision. If I had, I might not have made some of the decisions I did. This does not absolve the other party, for the way they behave is according to their own character, their beliefs and their past experiences. Even if they behave poorly, they will justify their behaviour, accept no responsibility and blame others. Consequently, arguing with them is pointless. It is best to walk away. They are responsible for the way they behave. I am responsible for the way I behave.

I am responsible for my choices, decisions
and outcomes.

In late 2009, we made a decision to return to Australia. Bill and Betty were furious that we were leaving Singapore yet we were expected to continue with the business in Australia. We chose Sydney because we felt it would be the best location for launching Bedrock Australia—the Australian equivalent of the Singapore business. We arrived in Sydney with enough money for two weeks' accommodation and that was it. Our only assets were shares in two unlisted companies, which had no value on the open market.

Never, ever put all your eggs in the one
basket and invest everything in the
one project.

We applied for Centrelink benefits and were rejected because when we left Australia we still had assets. We were able to borrow some more personal funds to enable us to eat, but accommodation was an issue. One of my friends, an osteopath just outside of Sydney, very generously offered to help by providing his clinic for us to live in. At night, we would sleep on the floor of his treatment rooms, then vacate these early in the morning, so he could run his practice. This was the lowest of the low. Five years earlier, I had been a successful plastic surgeon with my own clinics, living in a lovely home with my young family. I no longer could afford to pay the fees to keep my medical registration going. Similarly, the Melbourne Cricket Club membership I had so coveted was gone because I couldn't afford to keep up the yearly fees.

Stubbornness and resilience are commendable characteristics for most people. When combined with ego, as in my case, these characteristics might not always work in a person's best interests. Hence, going back to medicine was not an option for me. I decided to make Bedrock Australia work. This required purchasing another licence agreement from Bill and Betty's company. As Bedrock Australia had no funds, it was necessary to raise capital. I worked long and hard and eventually secured the first investment for Bedrock Australia. It was A$100,000 and I was so happy as I genuinely believed I could make the business work in Australia. I should have had a major rethink when the funds came in and Bill and Betty's company took 90 per cent of the funds.

Meanwhile, Fiona successfully applied for a job in the Sydney CBD. She was not due to start until the new year but I called a banking colleague with whom I had worked years before. Based on our relationship and the funds that would be coming in, Westpac agreed to loan us some money. This was a major breakthrough for we were able to secure an apartment to rent on the Pacific Highway closer to the city. Furthermore, we were able to release our furniture that had been in storage in Melbourne for four years. We moved into our new apartment on Christmas Eve 2009. As yet our furniture had not arrived so we had Christmas lunch at a card table sitting on camping chairs. Christmas presents and food were made possible because the only funds we could get came from the Salvation Army. It is ironic, that over the years, I had tithed thousands of dollars to the Army. A few years later, the only organisation who was there for us when we were in desperate need, was the same organisation.

Thank God for the Salvos.

My passion and commitment resulted in the business consuming me. I worked from 7am to 11pm (and often more) a minimum of six days a week. Most of that time was spent at the office so I rarely saw my family. We were a company that advocated work/life balance yet I had none. There was no regular salary. I often paid myself last which meant personal funds often trickled in. After a few years, I took on employees. This was a mistake and one of my regrets. Just because I was used to working for little or no funds did not mean employees should do the same. The employees were gracious, however, they did not receive the funds to which they were entitled and they should never have been put in this position.

Employees are a company's greatest asset
so always treat them with respect.

From the start, the change of career from plastic surgeon into business, had been a joint venture between Fiona and myself. We had both made the decision to invest in the businesses and both made the decision to move the family to Singapore. We had become co-directors of the Bedrock Singapore. I had spent a lot of time in Australia working for the Singapore business, Fiona had held increasingly responsible roles in Bedrock Singapore, culminating in her becoming the Managing Director. After our return to Australia, Fiona and I were co-directors of Bedrock Australia. Whilst things were very challenging for our family I made the assumption that we were doing this together and that even though things were very tough, together we would pull through. For me, marriage was a lifelong commitment and I believed this was true for Fiona as well.

However, the financial challenges were enormous and I was working at the office until 10pm most nights. In mid 2012, Fiona began to talk about separation. This was not something I wanted, however, we had used our previous separation to clarify that we both wanted to be together. I assumed that this would again be the case. There was no question in my mind that it would only be temporary.

It was therefore the greatest shock of my life to discover that Fiona was leaving the household—permanently. Late one Sunday night, I had an intuitive feeling that something was wrong. I then asked if she was leaving and was devastated and distraught to hear that she was leaving on Tuesday. I had assumed we were still working together in partnership and I could not have been more mistaken. I was heartbroken and I cried and cried. It seemed that everything I had believed in about marriage was crumbling around me. What of our children? Fiona was leaving by herself and Bek and Tim would be staying with me. Bek and Tim didn't even know about these plans at this stage, however, I was grateful they would be staying. I hated the fact that our family was breaking up.

The following day, Monday, was a work day. It was surreal. Fiona had decided she was leaving and nothing would change her mind. I had never ever considered that Fiona and I would not be together and this was the last day. I knew I would need to tell the kids. How do you prepare for that? Nobody teaches you this stuff. I felt so inadequate.

Arriving home from work I still had some hope this wasn't happening, however, after talking with Fiona, it was clear nothing had changed. Fiona had already rented a place and was moving in the following day. The children needed to be told. I am pretty much upfront in the things I say. If I feel a truth needs to be told, I have trouble withholding it. I would rather tell the truth and deal with the consequences, than withhold or tell half-truths that might have larger consequences at a later date.

When I called Bek and Tim to the lounge room, they were oblivious to what was about to happen and had no idea what I was going to say. Fiona and I had argued occasionally, usually about finances, in front of the children, however, our household was generally cohesive. We discussed things behind closed doors if necessary and fighting was a rarity.

To tell our children that their Mum was leaving the home the following day was by far, the hardest thing I have ever had to do. Tim was inconsolable. Bek was distraught, however, as I was to find out later, she had had her suspicions for a few months. I told them that both Fiona and I loved them very much and that Fiona was leaving me, not them. However, in the shock and upset of the moment I am not sure any of that was heard.

My heart was broken, yet now my children needed me more than ever. I have heard some say that children just want their parents to be happy. Yes, this is true, but if the parental relationship is not destructive, my opinion is that children want their parents to be together. Bek was 21, Tim 19. It doesn't matter how old children are when their parents separate, it causes a gut-wrenching, gaping hole that can never be completely healed.

The following day, after 23 years of marriage, I said goodbye to Fiona for the final time. When I came home early from work she was gone along with her belongings and some furniture. Bek, Tim and I sat on the floor, hugged each other and cried together. I wanted us all to be honest with how we were feeling, so we all took turns to share how we had been impacted. We got takeaway and kept going until we were exhausted.

One of the great benefits to emerge from a challenging situation was the deepening of my relationship with Bek and Tim. We were honest with each other. It was impossible to hide my hurt, however, I wanted them to know that I was strong, reliable and resilient and that together, we would come through. Within a few days, Fiona had gone away on holiday. Bek, Tim and I watched the AFL grand final on TV and although we bought the same junk food, it just wasn't the same without Mum. I left notes in the kitchen telling Bek and Tim that I loved them and that we would come through, together. About ten days later, Fiona and I met for the first time. I still hoped for reconciliation, however, it became clear this was not on the agenda.

Although I felt betrayed, hurt and at times angry, it was time for me to consider what had happened. If I was to learn from the situation, I had to pose and answer some tough questions. This is not easy to do when the first inclination is to act like a victim and blame the other person, however, there are always two sides and both people are responsible for the choices and actions they take. If I didn't accept my responsibility and learn from my mistakes, I would repeat the same mistakes if I ever had the opportunity in another relationship.

My first realisation was that I had taken Fiona for granted. I had expected her to make the most of our circumstances and simply be there. I also hadn't provided for her in the way she had wanted or expected. My change of career, my long working hours and financial difficulties had threatened her sense of security and I was not intuitive or caring enough to recognise that she had changed. She would say that she was telling me she was struggling, however, I wasn't listening to her. I made assumptions that she would always be there, that she would always be supportive and that she was still committed to the businesses. Further to this, I hadn't asked her the right questions. If

I had the courage, I would have checked in on a frequent basis with, 'How are you doing?' or 'Is this still working for you?' or 'What can I do to make things better?' I didn't ask these questions because I didn't want to hear the answers and simply carried on as though I was bulletproof. It was confronting to have these realisations about myself and I apologised to Fiona when I next saw her. I was deeply sorry I had put her in that situation and though the damage was already done in our relationship, I resolved never to behave in the same way again.

Never, ever take anyone for granted.

We resolved to remain friends. I truly wanted (and still want) the best for Fiona. However, it was clear she felt I was not the best person for her. We share 23 years of predominantly special memories and together we have raised two children who are outstanding human beings. Of this we can both be proud.

We arranged our own financial agreement and both applied for the dissolution of our Marriage. When this came through, after 25 years of marriage, there was a part of me that was sad, however, time and other events have a way of healing painful periods of life.

Fighting with a former spouse is selfish
and primarily impacts the children.

Back in the Game

The first Christmas without Mum was tough. Bek, Tim and I decided to have Christmas at home and we would do all the cooking ourselves. We bought the turkey and I stuffed it because Bek and Tim couldn't bring themselves to do anything quite so revolting as putting their hand up a turkey's clacker. (You can see why there is only one doctor in the family). Nevertheless, we had a lot of fun preparing the full Christmas dinner with trimmings. One of my Christmas presents from Bek and Tim was season one of *Game of Thrones*. After the traditional post lunch nap, I rather reluctantly watched the first episode of *Game of Thrones*. After one episode I was hooked and we watched the whole season straight through.

On Boxing Day, during the lunch break of the cricket, I was feeling a bit sorry for myself. On Christmas Eve I had been out with friends who had met online and were now married. I had now been separated for three months and reconciliation was increasingly unlikely. It was time to be considering the future so I thought it would be a good opportunity to explore online dating. This was a whole new world for me and it was with some trepidation that I viewed the eHarmony website. I had prepared my curriculum vitae several times in the past, however, preparing a profile that might be of some interest to another was a different ballgame. Furthermore, what should I be looking for in a woman? It was a long time since I had considered that question, but it was fairly important I get it right. It took me ages to complete the questionnaire, however, finally I was ready to get started. Just one more click! I did this and a notice flashed up to say that because I was separated, I was unable to participate in eHarmony. I was not happy because the website now had all my details and I was unable to use the site until I was divorced. The other option was to lie about my marital status, however, my aim was to be totally honest because trust was a significant issue for me. If I was trustworthy, it would be more likely my partner would be as well.

The only other site I knew was RSVP. And so began my venture into a world I never knew existed.

I was amazed just how many women of all ages had registered on the site. Presumably there were just as many men. Thank goodness it was a holiday, for it took hours to have even a brief look through. I decided to register and upload my profile. I was a complete newbie so I kept running everything by Bek. That must have been weird for her because I had not been in the habit of asking for dating advice from my daughter! After reading quite a few of the women's profiles, it was clear many were sick of jerks, particularly liars. It was clear they wanted men to be real and if they had some direction in life this was an advantage. My RSVP name was 'Passionate and Real'. I am not sure if that was a good name or not, however, I thought it summed me up. ('Desperate and Real' didn't seem quite so attractive!)

At this time, *Fifty Shades of Grey* had not yet hit the cinemas. However, it seemed that many women had read the book. I hadn't, however, I had some inkling of its content. One of the profiles that caught my eye was from a lady in her forties who focused on how much she enjoyed the book. Interestingly, when I read her profile the following day, it had changed. She was encouraging any potential suitors to read the book as well. It had been 25 years since I had dated another woman, so statements such as this I found intimidating. Nevertheless, I read a few pages of the book online just to familiarise myself. Now I was even more intimidated! One of the ways to overcome intimidation is to take action in spite of it. I made contact with '*Fifty Shades*' and we agreed to meet for dinner the following evening.

It was the penultimate night of the year and I was full of anticipation, with a touch of anxiousness. I was going on a date with another woman for the first time in 25 years. We had arranged to meet on a street corner. It is pretty easy to spot me. I am the bald guy. I didn't recognise the lady because she looked a little different to her profile photo. Dinner was enjoyable though disconcerting as I discovered that rather than being in her forties, she was actually in her sixties. A little later in the conversation, I, with some trepidation, raised the subject of her favourite book.

'Oh that,' she said. 'I am not that interested in the book, but I haven't been getting too many dates, so my girlfriend wrote the stuff about *Fifty Shades of Grey* and suggested I put it on my profile.'

Talk about an anticlimax!

Online dating profiles occasionally only
vaguely resemble the people behind them.

It was back to RSVP for me. My thought this time was that maybe dinner was not such a good idea for a first date. I connected with a woman that I arranged to meet for a drink in the city.

We had a lot of fun chatting about each other and our experiences. She had been online longer than I and she seemed a little warier. Wanting to know more about how it all worked, I said, 'Tell me, how do you work out if you want to see someone again?'

'You really want to know?' she asked warily.

'Sure,' I said. 'This is all new to me. I am fascinated.'

'Well,' she said. 'I work out very early on whether I want to give him a blow job or not.'

'You are joking?' I asked incredulously.

'No. Here's how it works. If the answer is yes, I definitely want to see him again. If the answer is no, there is no way I want to see him again. If the answer is maybe, then perhaps I will see him again.'

Thereafter, we stayed in touch by text for a while, however, I never got to find out which category I had fitted into.

Then there was the lady who I had arranged to meet for a morning coffee. I had arrived at the designated meeting place first. She walked in, said hello, sat down and placed her phone on the table. She then tapped her phone so it was playing background music. Clearly she had done this before! She then proceeded to ask me a series of questions with about as much enthusiasm as a student reciting their multiplication tables. I answered the first few then I had had enough.

'Stop,' I said raising my hand up. 'What are you doing?'

'I am just asking a few questions,' she said.

'Well you are not even listening to the answers,' I said. (It is not often a man gets to tell a woman she is not listening!)

'If you want to have a proper conversation, turn that thing off and we can talk. You know, like normal people,' I said.

It was as if I had woken her out of a stupor. She turned the phone off and proceeded to tell me she had been online for a long time and had become bored with the dating scene. Most guys were jerks and she expected me to be the same. After a while she relaxed and told me a little more about herself, as did I. She was a Mum and she agreed to come home to meet my children. I thought this was important as Bek and Tim knew I was dating, however, until then they had not met any of the women. She was great with Bek and Tim, laughing with them and reassuring them their Dad had not gone crazy.

I arranged to see her again, however, she refused to allow me to pick her up at her home. We had to meet in the street and I then drove her to the cinema. I took her arm to escort her, however, she had a rule that there could be no touching until we had been on a certain number of dates. She was intelligent, fun and great with children, however, I have struggled with rules at the best of times. I was looking for a relationship where the rules were a little more fluid.

I found that, in Bali. Through RSVP, I had begun talking with an expat who lived in Bali and I was due to travel there for an event. One evening, I arranged for a car to take me to her home and asked the driver to wait while we went out to dinner. Dinner was lovely and she seemed to be enjoying herself. I certainly was. When we returned to her home the driver was still waiting. I said I wouldn't be long, rather hoping I was mistaken.

Here I was, in a foreign country, with a lovely woman, to whom I was attracted and I wasn't sure what to do next.

After we had chatted a little longer, I said, 'I guess I should go, but I really don't want to.'

'You don't have to,' she said with only the hint of a smile.

Now, it might have been 25 years since I had been with another woman, however, I hadn't forgotten everything. I knew an opportunity when I saw one. I temporarily excused myself, spoke with the driver telling him I wouldn't be requiring his services for the rest of the night and would find my own way home.

Whilst this whole experience was exciting, I also felt a bit sad. I had never wanted or expected to be in a situation like this and I felt myself dealing with a mixture of passion and guilt. Fortunately, passion won out and we had a lot of fun. I stayed with her for a few days after the event and I invited her to come out to Sydney to stay a few days. A few months later she did indeed come out to stay at our place. If I had my time again, I would have done it differently. It was less than six months since the separation, and for me to have invited another woman into the home is something I regret. It was ill considered and selfish. It is one thing to have a rebound relationship, however, it would have been better to not involve the children. In spite of its short nature, this was the relationship I needed at that time. I learned that I wasn't washed up, that I was still attractive and that I had plenty to offer another woman.

Sometimes a short-term relationship is just
what we need.

The Doctor Becomes a Patient

A few months later, I woke as usual around 5am and went for my run around the boardwalk of Sydney harbour. The waterfront is one of the most spectacular sites in the world and running along its edge was one of the highlights of my day. My morning routine includes planning my day. This includes writing out my vision, goals and to do list. As I was writing I noticed my handwriting looked a little strange. I quickly passed this off as I was still sweating from my run. I then proceeded with my affirmations which I would speak out loud each day to reinforce what was important to me, particularly the character traits I wanted to emulate. I was a little startled when I was unable to correctly pronounce the word 'honourable'. I initially thought this might be because I had not been honourable, however, impairment of my fine motor skills required for writing along with my speech was a little disconcerting. When I got into the shower and couldn't feel with one side of my hand while I was washing myself, I became concerned. There was no history of cerebrovascular disease in my family, I was fit, healthy and had never had symptoms like this before. Under many circumstances, in typical doctor fashion when dealing with our own health, I might have downplayed the symptoms, thinking this is probably a Transient Ischaemic Attack (TIA) and will pass, however, I had enough common sense to call a local GP clinic to make an appointment for a few hours time.

It was a 15-minute walk to the GP's clinic, uphill all the way. When I arrived, I explained my symptoms, which were still persisting, to the doctor. My pulse and blood pressure were normal, I felt fine and I expected him to send me off home. Instead he told me to get my butt up to the Royal North Shore Hospital.

'When?' I enquired.

'NOW!' he replied. 'You are probably having a stroke. Shall I call an ambulance?'

I arrived at the emergency department of the Royal North Shore Hospital by taxi. After a brief triage I was immediately changed into a hospital gown, placed on a hospital gurney, had a drip inserted and became a public patient of the system in which I had trained. Every aspect of my treatment was first class. By that evening I had had a CT scan, an MRI scan, various blood tests and I was diagnosed with a left thalamic stroke. As I was waiting to have one of the scans, I thought I should tell my children. But what do I say without having them alarmed? 'Hi Bek and Tim, not to worry but Dad's having a stroke and if I get out of hospital alive, I might be permanently disabled,' did not seem right. Fortunately, Bek contacted Fiona who slipped into nurse mode, got the children together, explained what was happening and prepared them for how I might look in hospital. Fiona was terrific and for a short time the family was back together. It was just that the emergency department was not the ideal location for a family reunion!

I was admitted to the neurological ward where I was the youngest patient by about 20 years. My symptoms disappeared over a 24-hour period, however, I was kept in hospital in order to explore what might have caused the stroke. A stroke is where a part of the brain dies due to a lack of blood supply. This might be caused by a bleed into the brain, often as the result of trauma or weak walls of the blood vessels, or where a clot lodges in a blood vessel, preventing blood from getting through. In my case, the most likely cause was a clot, however, it was not clear where it had originated. My heart was healthy, as were the major blood vessels in my neck. My cholesterol was a littler high and there was an unusual antibody detected, however, everything else was clear. A subsequent CT scan of the heart showed that I had a calcium score of zero meaning there was no detectable plaque on the blood vessels around my heart. The cause for my stroke, if that what it was, still remains an enigma.

Our health is our greatest asset and
should never be taken for granted.

Whilst these tests were being performed, I made myself useful in the ward by providing assistance to the other patients. The nursing care was first class though it was those who showed a little more caring, with a kind word or a simple touch that stood out to me. It was a very different experience as a doctor to be in a bed rather than standing at the end of one. Firstly, to see a doctor is very gratifying. I know that nowadays there is a tendency for surgeons, in particular, to have their nurses see the patient postoperatively in hospital. My personal experience is that it is a different feeling when seen by a doctor. It is reassuring and respectful. In my opinion it is a task that should not be delegated. When a doctor is visiting, there is a marked difference between those who stand at the end of the bed, waxing lyrical, and those who come to the side of the bed or even sit on it. Simple acts like that, demonstrate more care, more understanding and more empathy. They are also more likely to be recommended to the patient's friends. In other words, it costs nothing, the patient feels cared for and it has enormous benefits.

After three nights in hospital, I was ready to go home. My symptoms had resolved completely within the first 24 hours and I was incredibly fortunate to have no residual defect. When the neurologist visited me before discharge, he showed me my MRI scan, which clearly demonstrated a black spot in the left thalamic area of the brain. In all the tests that had been completed, no cause had been found. He said that some people referred to the Thalamus as representing a person's 'soul'. I asked if stress could play a causative role and he denied this to be the case.

I beg to differ. Within the previous 12 months, I had lost a great deal of money and frequently lived well below the poverty line, my wife had left, I had moved house, the business in Singapore had failed and the Australian business was heading the same way. Along with that, I had been dealing with several businesses related legal issues (even whilst I was in hospital). Any one of these factors are well known causes of acute stress. Putting them all together produces a concoction of acute chronic stress. If one of my own patients had been going through that, I would think that damage to a persons' 'soul' is not an unexpected outcome.

Stress significantly compromises a
person's health.

Once I was home I researched cerebrovascular disease to ascertain what changes I might implement in order to prevent any recurrence of my symptoms. Whilst in hospital I had been placed on low dose aspirin to thin my blood and statins to lower my cholesterol. I was comfortable remaining on aspirin and have continued to take it to this day. However, as a young doctor, I had been sceptical of the role cholesterol was said to play in disease of the arteries. Nevertheless, I was not against reducing my slightly elevated cholesterol. I just wanted to be off statins as soon as I could.

Previously, I had been a vegetarian for several years. Although I enjoy meat, it is not something I have to have and my reading indicated, becoming a vegetarian once again might be of advantage. Along with this, I decided, where possible, to only eat organic food. This entailed weekly trips to an organic market to buy fresh vegetables, however, this became fun as I got to know some of the produce sellers. Furthermore, I visited my local health food shop and spoke with the proprietor, a fully trained naturopath. She encouraged my organic and vegetarian lifestyle and also added that I would be better to refrain from caffeine. Again, I had done this previously so returning to decaffeinated coffee and tea was not difficult. However, there are two ways of treating coffee to remove the caffeine. One way is using chemicals, which many have said is more harmful than the caffeine itself. Another is using water to extract the caffeine, the so-called Swiss method. This is preferred as it is said to be more natural.

Many think that decaffeinated coffee loses its taste. In fact, I have heard stories, hopefully apocryphal, that some baristas, who don't stock decaf, will serve weak normal coffee, representing it as decaf. I like my coffee strong and black and when this is first class decaf, it is impossible to distinguish from normal coffee. When I would ask at restaurants if they served decaf coffee treated with the Swiss method, the best waiters and baristas would know instantly. Nowadays most good restaurants stock water based decaf coffee, however, if you are not sure, ask.

Within two months of commencing an organic vegetarian (primarily vegan) diet along with decaf coffee, I had lost 10kg and my cholesterol had dropped dramatically to be in the normal range. I came off the statins and have not been back on them since.

Whilst I had addressed my diet, I was still under considerable stress. Money had dried up, I was behind in my rent and the legal issues with Bedrock Australia would not go away. I needed to do something different otherwise the next health crisis might not be so temporary.

At this stage I was responsible for Bedrock Australia with its 50 shareholders and others who had loaned money to the company. Because many of these people were personal friends or people I had come to know well, I found it very difficult to acknowledge the business was failing. I believed in the company, its mission and purpose. However, belief does not put food on the table and my business venture had cost me my marriage, my savings and now my health. Something needed to change.

We are personally responsible for
reducing stress in our lives.

Back to Plastic Surgery

I was contemplating this whilst sitting in one of my favourite parks overlooking Sydney Harbour. I was quite mindlessly checking my Facebook feed, when an advertisement for an Australian plastic surgeon to work in Dubai, literally jumped off the page. It was offering a salary similar to what I had once enjoyed. I had now been out of medicine for six years and I had never seriously considered returning. To me it would be a sign that I had failed in the business venture. This, of course, had already happened, though I was yet to admit it to myself. I assumed the only way to return to medicine would be if I sat an exam, which might be a little daunting. But what if I could return? It could certainly improve my personal financial situation and maybe I could even finance the business.

I made enquiries about the Dubai position and discovered they preferred someone who was currently practicing. I also explored a couple of other non-surgical options in Australia and found there were various positions for which I had the experience and could manage without any further training. I then began to consider something I had not previously contemplated. 'What if I could go back to plastic surgery in Australia? Is that possible? If so, what would I need to do?'

The answers were quite simple. Firstly, I needed to regain my medical registration which I had let slip several years previously when I didn't have the funds to pay for the renewal premium. The Medical Board now came under the auspices of the Australian Health Practitioners Registration Authority (AHPRA). I rang AHPRA, explained I had allowed my registration to lapse six years previously and that I would now like to return to full registration to practise surgery. I was staggered to find that I simply needed to fill out an application form which would be considered by the Medical Board and that I might have some restrictions placed on my registration for 12 months or so. However, there did not seem to be any issue in the way of me re-entering practice. I would require a letter from the Royal Australian College of Surgeons (RACS) confirming I was qualified to practise along with one or two colleagues who would be willing to act as referees.

Next I rang the RACS to explain my situation. Surprisingly, they appeared delighted I was re-entering practice and sent me the necessary letters the same day. So far so good and it had been amazingly easy.

I then had to consider that if I were to practise again as a plastic surgeon, what would that look like? To recommence in solo practice, would take up front cash and time to build. I had neither. It would be logical to practise in Melbourne, however, I now lived in Sydney. I didn't want to live in Melbourne but perhaps I could travel there? Eight years previously, whilst living in Singapore, I had travelled to Australia to consult and operate. Perhaps it was still possible to live in one state and commute to another to work? What if I lived in Sydney and worked in Melbourne and Queensland, both places in which I had worked previously?

These were some of the thoughts going through my mind when I called my colleague, Dr Mark Vucak. I was excited because I could sense that not only was there a way out of the predicament I had created for myself, it might even be possible to prosper. I told myself not to get too carried away for there was a long way to go. Nevertheless, some light at the end of a very long tunnel is way better than complete blackness.

Mark is a plastic surgeon who had grown his business, Queensland Plastic Surgery, into one of the largest practices in Australia. Based in Townsville, he had also built large practices in Rockhampton and Mackay. We had known each other for more than 20 years and he had welcomed me into his practice when I was first separated from my wife in 2006. He had called a few years later to ask when I was coming back to plastic surgery. At that time, I had laughed and told him that wouldn't be happening. Consequently, I wasn't quite sure how he would respond. I need not have been worried. Mark was delighted to hear I was returning to plastic surgery and would make space available for me to consult and operate in Rockhampton and Townsville. We talked about the revenue he expected me to generate for a commitment of one week a month and for someone who was struggling to pay the rent, the amount seemed staggering. Furthermore, he would send me a contract along with an offer of employment that I could forward to AHPRA, my medical insurers and to some financial institutions to hopefully facilitate a loan.

Next, I rang my plastic surgical colleague, Dr Craig Rubinstein in Melbourne. Craig and I had also known each other for more than 20 years and he had also grown his business, Cosmetic Surgery for Women, into one of the largest practices in Australia. The timing was perfect for Craig as he was just moving into larger, fully renovated rooms and was looking to expand his practice. Interestingly his new rooms were a stone's throw from one of my previous practice locations. He welcomed me back to plastic surgery and he would be very happy for me to join his practice. Both Mark and Craig were willing to act as referees should AHPRA require this.

Life's events can change very quickly. Just two days previously, I was at one of my lowest ebbs and my position had seemed hopeless. Now I had positive responses from AHPRA, the RACS, my previous medical insurer and I had offers to work with experienced plastic surgeons in highly reputable practices.

I submitted my application form to AHPRA and waited. I was told it would take at least a month for the Medical Board to consider my application and notify me of my success or otherwise. After a month I called and emailed. Still no response. Another week went by. Then a second. I was beginning to worry, though there was nothing further I could do.

On 6 November 2013, I received an email advising that the NSW Registration Committee of the Medical Board of Australia had considered my application for specialist registration. They noted my previous registration and practice history; my gap in clinical practice since December 2006 and that I had not undertaken any continuing professional development during this gap in practice. Nevertheless, as my membership of the Royal Australasian College of Surgeons had been reactivated, *the committee had agreed to approve my application for registration* subject to eight conditions that outlined a gradual return to practice, over a 12-month period, under the supervision of referees approved by the board.

In other words, I was free to re-enter medical practice and as long as I met certain conditions, I could once again practice as a plastic surgeon.

This was one of my greatest moments. I had been through a personal hell and I had now taken the first steps to regaining some equilibrium, some dignity, some personal belief and some confidence...not to mention some cash! I was excited, relieved and overwhelmingly grateful for the opportunity to return to the profession that had been so good to me. I felt a bit like the prodigal son in the biblical story, who took his inheritance, wasted it and was ashamed to have lost everything. It was only when he had reached rock bottom that he acknowledged his poor decisions and humbly decided to return to his family home. He was then overwhelmed to find his father waiting for him with open arms. This is how I felt. I was humble and grateful. I resolved never to take anything worthwhile for granted ever again.

No matter the problem, there is always
a solution.

Reunion With Old Friends

Whilst I was waiting for the approval from AHPRA, I thought of Wesley. Though he had crossed my mind several times over the years, I had not seen him in almost 20 years. I was unaware of his whereabouts or his wellbeing and with my imminent return to plastic surgery, I was curious as to what had happened to him. When I had last seen Wesley there was no such thing as Facebook and mobile phones were only possessed by the privileged few. It was now 2013 and one of my friends on Facebook was Colin Smith who was the coordinator of all the logistics for 'Operation Wesley'. If anybody would know about Wesley, it would be Colin. I messaged him on Facebook and shortly thereafter received a reply which stunned me. Wesley was not only alive and well, he was working for the Salvation Army…in Sydney! He was living and working just a few kilometres from where I was living. He was apparently living with Lorraine, the Major from the Salvation Army, who knew Wesley as a little boy in Papua New Guinea. She was the person who had first contacted me and initiated the whole process.

I was so excited. Making a difference in people's lives is at my core and there had been very little of that over the past few years. To consider that there was a young man who was living a meaningful life and contributing to society as a result of the skills I had been taught, was very fulfilling. For me it was a confirmation that I was doing the right thing by moving back into surgery.

I called Lorraine and she was excited to hear from me. She knew that Wesley would be very happy to see 'Uncle Malcolm' and we arranged to meet the following week. When I had last seen Wesley he would rarely speak to me so I was unsure how he would respond to me after almost 20 years. I needn't have worried. When we met he greeted me with a hug and we shook hands, left handed, as we had always done. He was a fine young man, taller of course, than when we had last met, and he spoke with affection and a dry sense of humour. He explained that he hadn't wanted to talk with me as a boy, because to him I represented pain. Nowadays he had been adopted by Lorraine, was living in Sydney, and enjoying working for the Salvation Army. He was in touch with his family and they were well but he hadn't been back to PNG for several years. It was surreal talking with him. His head was upright and though the scars from his multiple surgeries were still evident, he had now grown dreadlocks (which made me jealous) and to me his face was beautiful. I couldn't help but think of the night we had first met, with the side of his face melted to his chest and me thinking, 'What am I going to do here?' Now he was talking, laughing, expressing and just being a normal, fun-loving young man. He even insisted on paying for drinks. It was immensely rewarding for me. In those few minutes, Wesley gave to me more than I could ever imagine.

When we give to others, we often get back
more than we could ever expect.

Towards the end of our conversation, Wesley explained he was having a few issues with the front of his neck. One of the procedures Mr Michael Leung had performed involved taking a block of tissue from his back and inserting it into his neck to enable him greater flexibility. This had worked well, however, the block of tissue was quite bulky so Wes had trouble finding a collar that was large enough for his neck. He asked if I might be able to do something for him to make this easier. At that stage I had not heard if I would still be able to regain my Medical Registration, however, I promised that if I did, I would be in touch and we could do something for him.

A few days later, I regained my registration and a few days thereafter, I travelled to Townsville for my first day back in medical practice. The conditions imposed on my return to practice were I believe, carefully considered for a medical practitioner and surgeon who had not held a scalpel for seven years. For the first two weeks I could only observe. After that time, I could consult with patients but only when my supervisor was close at hand. Thereafter, I could also assist at operations. This is an ideal way for a surgeon to regain some of the technical skill, such as suturing, without being the primary surgeon responsible for the patient's outcome. To be back in an operating theatre was a surreal experience. It was like returning to the family home, that I had lived in for 20 years, but was now owned by somebody else. It was exciting yet I initially felt quite self-conscious and cautious lest I contaminate a sterile area, which would be really embarrassing. I soon overcame my misgivings and came to appreciate the working environment. In the past I had taken the teamwork in the operating theatre for granted. Wrapped up in my own self-importance, I had paid scant attention to the anaesthetist, assistant surgeons, nursing staff, theatre technicians and administrative staff. All play their role and perhaps for the first time, I could clearly see that a surgeon is only as good as his team. A surgeon does his best work when he or she is relaxed. A friendly, professional and efficient team make this possible and as a peripheral observer I could now see this all playing out.

*The best service is provided by a team
committed to excellence.*

In the early weeks, the logistics of working in Townsville, Rockhampton and Mackay were somewhat taxing. I knew it would be a few months until I would be generating any revenue so I had to borrow funds to pay for flights, some accommodation and food. In Townsville, Mark had arranged for me to live in a room in an abandoned commercial building that was shared with a couple of young guys. For weeks I lived in a small room, with a camp stretcher for a bed, and a creaky fan above my head. Mice would occasionally run across the threadbare carpet. November and December in Townsville are hot and humid. Without air-conditioning, sleeping at night was occasionally challenging, however, each night I took comfort knowing it was only a matter of time until I could upgrade my accommodation. Each weekend I would fly home to Sydney to spend time with Bek and Tim. It might have saved some money to stay in Queensland, however, it always felt grounding to be at home, if just for a few days.

*When we are certain of a great outcome,
temporary inconvenience is just
that, temporary.*

I'm Back

After a month of observing, assisting and supervised consultation, I operated on my first patient. The patient required a skin cancer removed from his face and this was done in the rooms under local anaesthetic. In my early practice years, I had removed hundreds of similar skin cancers, however, I would be less than truthful if I did not say there was some level of trepidation associated with the first time I had picked up a scalpel in seven years. One of my plastic surgical colleagues used to say that it took an enormous amount of courage and self-confidence to make any incision on anybody's face at any time. This is true and never more so than on this day. Nevertheless, I discovered that there are some skills that are embedded deep in the memory banks. Movements of my fingers and hands seemed to flow in a way that surprised me. I was a little rusty, however, when I stopped thinking about what to do next, I just seemed to know. There was an unconscious competence in the way I drew around the lesion, injected local anaesthetic, prepped and draped, held the scalpel and applied the pressure required to cut, the way I sutured the wound edge and how many sutures I used etc. All the fine details that I had been taught, learned and practised over 20 years came flooding back in a way that simply amazed me.

From that first experience, I progressed to more excisions, then more complicated procedures for skin cancers, closing the defect with a flap or skin graft. All these were still under local anaesthetic in the rooms, however, it was not long until I had to see patients who required larger procedures under general anaesthetic in hospital. These patients were initially placed at the end of Mark's lists, so he could watch over me, however, shortly thereafter I had my very own operating list for my patients with skin cancer. This was quite a thrill for me as it was almost seven years to the day since my last operating list. It was another step on the way back and I was loving it.

When skills become unconsciously
competent, the knowledge never leaves us.

In early January 2014, I travelled to Melbourne to work with my colleague Dr Craig Rubinstein. In Melbourne, I initially stayed with my sister and brother-in-law, Denise and Darren Waterworth. Denise, Darren and their family, Ben, Annie and Jake, had supported me without judgement or question throughout my challenges over the previous few years. They were solid and grounded and when I felt as if my whole world was falling apart, their love and practical support gave me some security and stability.

> *Family members and others who love*
> *without condition, without judgement,*
> *are priceless.*

Craig liked to start the new year with a bang, so had scheduled an operating list each day from Monday to Friday and I was invited to assist him. This was exceptional experience as his patients were primarily cosmetic and I was able to observe and assist him, which brought me up to speed with cosmetic cases very quickly. Whilst the fundamentals of cosmetic surgery had changed little while I was away, two things stood out for me. The first was the quality of the anaesthetics had improved, so that patients woke up quicker, with less pain. It was also unusual for them to have nausea and vomiting postoperatively. This meant that more than one procedure could be performed at the one time. The rise of the so called 'Mummy makeover'—where mothers want to regain their pre-pregnancy bodies with combined procedures on their tummies and breasts—were now commonplace. Secondly, the procedure of breast enlargement had become way more popular. This was not only true for younger women but also for mums who had lost their breast tissue following pregnancy and breastfeeding. Many of these mums not only wanted their breasts to be back to their pre-

pregnancy size, but also wanted their droopy breasts lifted. This is known as an augmentation mastopexy. In my early practice, if this was performed it was usually done as a two-stage procedure requiring two operations and two anaesthetics. Now the procedures were usually combined adding complexity to the procedure, however, minimising the downtime for working mothers.

This was a period during which I experienced teamwork at its finest. Craig had surrounded himself with an outstanding team. Dr Andrew Rubinfeld his anaesthetist, Trish McCristal (who had worked as Craig's scrub nurse for more than 15 years and became known as the 'best scrub nurse in the world') and the supporting nursing staff and theatre technicians at the St Vincent's Private Hospital in Kew were all exceptional in their roles, which meant the patients received first class service. For me, it was even more like coming home. Thirty years previously, whilst still a trainee, I had assisted Mr Murray Stapleton at what was then the Vimy Private Hospital. His scrub nurse at the time, Joy Miller, was now in charge of theatres, so for me it felt very comfortable. Twenty years previously, Craig had come to my operating theatre to watch me perform and abdominoplasty. Now, I was assisting him, doing the same.

The Bedrock Sandcastle Collapses

In early 2014, whilst I was re-entering plastic surgery, I was still working with Bedrock Australia. Bedrock Australia had attracted clients from several Australian states, New Zealand and Singapore, and events had been delivered in Sydney and Perth. Our aim had been to develop Bedrock Centres in Australia's major cities from which the events would be delivered. The plan was based on Bedrock Singapore's business plan, prepared by Bill. As with Singapore, a minimum of 50 per cent of the capital raised in Australia was forwarded to Bill and Betty's company in order to purchase the licence agreement for Australia. They valued this at A$2 million. It took until early 2013 to complete this payment, but complete it we did. I then requested the licence agreement be forwarded. This was never done. Instead, Bedrock Australia received another invoice for several hundred thousand dollars from Bill along with various threats. It was then, that I knew the business relationship had broken down irretrievably.

I sought independent advice from corporate experts who told me the business plan was flawed and was only designed for Bill's benefit. Much of what I had believed had been a lie. It was crushing. Unknowingly, the shareholders and investors of Bedrock Singapore and Bedrock Australia had funded Bill and Betty's lifestyle and the prime assets of the companies—the licence agreements—were worthless. I spoke with our lawyers and it was their suggestion that Bedrock Australia be placed in administration. This was an extremely difficult decision for me to make for it was an admission of failure and meant that many good people would lose their money. Many of these people were my friends. I believed in the company and its vision and people had believed in me. It was a painful period and it is a huge regret that I recommended an investment to friends in a project that failed. However, I know, beyond a shadow of a doubt, that I, and many others, gave everything we had to make the project in Singapore and Australia work. Unfortunately, the project itself was flawed and only designed to benefit one entity.

If a plan is fundamentally flawed, no
amount of hard work can rescue it.

Bedrock Australia was placed into administration in mid 2014. Whilst this was a major disappointment, when it finally occurred, it was somewhat of a relief. The subsequent shareholder meetings were relatively straightforward. Most of the shareholders gave me their proxies so I was prepared for anything Bill put forward. He was, however, quite subdued as I suspect he knew there was little gain for him and he potentially had a lot more to lose if there was any dispute.

At its close, the company had loans and convertible notes from investors totalling $1.6 million. The vast majority of these investors accepted their responsibility for the investment. Most of them were friends or people I had come to know and I decided I could and would do something about it. Although there was no legal obligation, I felt a moral obligation and I made a personal commitment to myself to repay these investors the full amount of $1.6 million. This will take me ten years to complete but complete it I will. Unfortunately, all the shareholders, including myself lost their money. However, those who loaned money to the company will have their principal repaid. I feel it is the right thing to do.

Doing the right thing might not be
comfortable, but it is still the right thing.

Back to 60 Minutes

Meanwhile, I continued to assist Craig and it occurred to me that it might be possible to perform Wesley's next procedure at St Vincent's Private Hospital in Kew. This is a Catholic hospital and I was aware that they occasionally provided free healthcare in special circumstances. I mentioned Wesley to Joy and she was favourable to the idea of doing his operation at the hospital. Further discussions with the hospital administrators were also favourable so a plan was beginning to take shape.

I also began to wonder if *60 Minutes* might be interested in picking up the story again. I was always curious as to why the story had never gone to air. I knew that *60 Minutes* had some fabulous footage and I believed Wesley's story would be one that Australians would appreciate. I decided to give Channel 9 a call. I remembered Stephen Taylor's name, the producer of the original story. I thought it was unlikely he was still part of the show, however, I asked for him. To my great surprise and delight, Stephen came on the phone. Some 20 years later, he was still producing stories for *60 Minutes* and he remembered Wesley and myself very well. The first thing he did was apologise for the story never having gone to air. He said he had thought of me often and was embarrassed he had not contacted me. He explained that the challenge with the original story was that Wesley was unable to talk to the camera so it was felt the television audience might not warm to him. An executive decision had been made to scrap the story, so it had never gone to air.

He asked what I had been up to and in a few minutes I summarised my experiences over the last 20 years. I explained I had just returned to surgery and that recently I had met up with Wesley. He was delighted to hear so, and asked how Wesley was. I explained how well he was doing and also mentioned that he was very communicative and expressive. Stephen sounded a little doubtful initially, however, I assured him Wesley was a pretty typical young man, a little shy, but fun-loving and warm. I also explained Wesley had asked if I could do further work on him, and that I was planning for that to be done in Melbourne. Would *60 Minutes* be interested in picking up the story?

From a personal perspective, Stephen told me he would love to do this. He had always felt the story was incomplete and he would like to film Wesley returning to his family in PNG with me there at the same time. However, there were two potential problems. Whilst the story was close to his heart, he wasn't sure this would be the case for those who made the executive decisions. Secondly, he wasn't sure if the original footage still existed as it was usually destroyed after a period of time. He did, however, promise to look for the footage, run it by the Executive Producer, and then get back to me.

Stephen called me back the following week with some good news. Remarkably they had found all the original footage gathering dust in one of Channel 9's dungeons. It would need to be converted into current day format but this was doable. Secondly his Executive Producer was keen to continue the story. This was great news. The proviso was that Stephen would like to have a chat with Wesley first, see him in his work environment and be certain Wes was interested in the story going to air. This he did and when he contacted me again he felt confident that the unfinished story could finally be completed.

*Sometimes a delay in a project can have
an even better outcome than expected.*

Picking Up the Pieces

During this time, I was still finding my feet in plastic surgery. For the first couple of months of 2014, it was not unusual for me to sit in the rooms and not see a patient all day. However, I felt it important for the staff to get to know me and I them, so that when a patient did make an enquiry, they were more likely to recommend they see me. Two of the first patients I saw were former patients I had operated on more than 20 years previously. One had a facelift and the other a breast augmentation. It was such a buzz to see two former patients who had sought me out online and made appointments to see me. The lady with the facelift was delighted with her result and felt that after 20 years she might benefit from a bit more work. This was my pleasure to do later that year. The other lady had had children since her operation, so her breasts were now droopier than she would have liked. Her result was still good, however, I suspect she will be back in the near future for a breast uplift. Seeing these patients meant that I could judge my previous work and my conclusion was that they were the right procedures for the right people at the right time. This was personally very gratifying.

One of the challenges was that whilst I had 15 years of experience in private practice in Melbourne, having seen thousands of patients over that time, all of the patient details along with my records now belonged to another entity, having been sold along with my practice. All my before and after photographs were in a storage unit to which I had no access. Craig's business manager, big Dave Staughton, came up with a great idea to offer minimal-cost surgery to family and friends. This was a win-win. It would allow me to build up my operating experience with a warm group of patients, whilst providing a service for those who might otherwise not be able to afford it. Each patient agreed to allow their pre and postoperative photographs to be shown to other patients. In this way I was able to do a few abdominoplasties (tummytucks), mastoplexies (breast lifts) and breast implant exchanges. The latter procedure is a common operation nowadays as many women, after ten years or more, want their implants exchanged for newer models. Whilst breast implants are now much safer than ever before, with the silicone gel designed to be cohesive so it doesn't leak, it is best to exchange them before they wear out. Some women use the opportunity to go a little larger and some a little smaller. Women have far more choice than at any time in history and this is true for their bodies. It is my recommendation to women to be clear about their choices, find a well-qualified surgeon they are comfortable with, and explore whether he or she can give them what they want.

Where your body is concerned, don't
compromise on quality.

Once I had become settled with consulting, I found my consulting style was vastly different to how it had been ten years previously. Then, I saw myself as the all-knowing expert who would spend a lot of time telling people about a procedure and its possible complications. Patients expect their surgeons to be experts and information about procedures is important so they can make well-informed decisions. It was a reasonable strategy because I had many happy patients and I was proud of the fact I had never been sued. However, I didn't spend much time listening to my patients. I had a spiel I wanted to complete in order to tick the legal boxes, so when a patient was talking, I wasn't listening attentively.

Now, perhaps because of my business experience, the personal development work I had done and the breakdown of my marriage, I found I was asking more questions and actually listening to the answers. I had come to realise that if they have the available funds patients will move forward providing they *trust* their surgeon. If they like their surgeon and the surgeon likes them, then that is an added bonus. Patients know there are potential complications with any surgical procedure. If they don't know this, they are not good candidates for surgery. There is so much information available on the internet and in social media and magazines that it is unusual for a patient to have not done at least some research before they make an appointment. Most importantly, they want to know that at all times the surgeon will act in their best interests, and if something does go wrong, the surgeon will not abandon them. This is where the trust comes in. The most successful surgeons always do the right thing by their patients, and if patients know that, they are more likely to move forward with an operation. This also works when an experienced surgeon says he or she cannot give the patient the result they are after. Surgeons love to operate. If a successful and trustworthy surgeon says no, it is wise to listen!

Patients want to trust their surgeons.

Consequently, after welcoming a new patient, asking them how I can help and making sure they are fit and healthy, I will say the following:

'My aim is for you to get a great result. I want you to be really happy. The best way I know to do that is firstly for me to get clear on what you want. For, if I give you what you want, you are more likely to be happy. Isn't that right? If I don't think I can give you what you want, I will tell you and find someone else who can give that to you.

So, with that in mind, I am going to draw you out a little more. I want you to describe for me your ideal outcome from the operation. What is it that you want?'

I then shut up and listen!

Most have been thinking about this for a long time, though they might never have expressed it. If they are struggling a little, I can ask a few more questions to help. Often the things that are said are similar.

For instance, one of the most common things I hear is from mothers, who effectively say, 'I love my children…and I want my body back!' When I first started practice in the 1990s, most women put up with the changes pregnancy had on their bodies (droopy and/or empty breasts, loose abdominal skin, stretch marks and particularly a bulge in the lower part of the tummy that seems completely resistant to diet and exercise). The 'matronly' look was an accepted way of being. Mums didn't like it but they tolerated it. Nowadays, things have changed. Women are educated, often have a career and are having children later in life. They have their own source of income and with it, more choice. The other major change over the last 25 years is the use of social media and with it the overwhelming focus on image. On any one day, our image can be uploaded to the internet, whether we have initiated this through our own selfies or someone else taking our photograph, with or without our consent. Celebrities and sports stars can make millions from perfect images uploaded to social media or viewed in magazines. Female celebrities celebrate their post pregnancy bodies, often without the acknowledgement of any surgical assistance. 'Normal' women the world over, whether consciously or unconsciously, are impacted by this all pervasive presence and want to look their best as much as possible. As cosmetic surgery has become more socially acceptable, more and more women are making an informed choice to do something for themselves.

More than at any time in history, women are choosing to regain their pre-pregnancy bodies.

For many women this is not an easy decision to make. By the time they are sitting in my office, no matter how calm they look, they often have two overwhelming feelings: terror and guilt. They are terrified of dying under the anaesthetic. Even if they have had previous surgical procedures, this is often the first time they have *chosen* to have an anaesthetic. Previous operations have usually been necessary for medical conditions and this is easily justified, however, a choice to undergo a cosmetic procedure puts the responsibility for the decision making primarily with the patient. It is not something she has to have; it is something she wants. In her mind she is putting herself at risk and what happens if something goes wrong? What happens if she dies? Who will raise her children? Is it fair to expect her husband to raise the children when she put herself at risk when this was not necessary?

Compounding the terror is guilt. Mums typically put the children and family first. Perhaps for the first time in her life, she is planning to spend a large amount of money on herself. This money could otherwise be allocated to school fees, a family holiday, a new car or the mortgage. Instead, she is focusing on herself and she feels guilty about this.

Most women will not say this, however, most of them are thinking and feeling along these lines. If I sense it will help, I will share the above and ask if they identify with any of what I have just said. Some tear up. Others are simply relieved that somebody understands what they are going through.

When contemplating surgery most mothers experience fear and guilt.

The vast majority of women I have seen in my practice, are not vain. In my understanding, vanity is when somebody compares himself or herself to another person and thinks they are better or wants to be better than them. However, wanting to look and feel good about yourself is not being vain. In response to my question, 'What is it that you want?', most will say they want to be able to fill out a top, or wear a backless/strapless dress, or wear more fitted clothes around their tummy or fit into a pair of jeans without bulging out the top. Most want to look good in their clothes as they are sick of wearing clothes to cover up their perceived flaws. If they look good naked that is a bonus.

When I am clear on what they want, I will then ask, 'When you have got that, what will that give you?'

They overwhelming answer, for women of all ages and all walks of life, is 'confidence!'

Often, women come to the consultation with their husbands or partners. It is not easy for the men for they might have similar feelings and are unsure what to make of the whole process. I have found the women who are the most ready for these procedure are those whose husbands/partners have said (and meant it) that, 'I love you as you are. For me, you don't need to change. However, if this is what you want, I will support you fully.' There is a lot of strength and security in a relationship where that kind of support is felt by the woman. In my experience, the men who do not want their partners to proceed with surgery have a control issue or a personal lack of confidence and are concerned that when their partners get what they want, they will leave the relationship for someone else.

When a woman has told me what she wants and expressed her fears, it is important for me to allay them. I reassure her that she will come through the anaesthetic. Yes, there are risks with every anaesthetic, however, the risk is very small. In fact, she has more risk of dying in a car accident, however, she will still get in her car and drive home. Furthermore, when she has recovered and she has achieved the result she wants, she will feel more confident, feminine and sexy. Apart from herself the biggest beneficiary is her husband or partner, closely followed by her children. The children might even be unaware that Mum has had something done, yet they will pick up on her increase in confidence. A woman who feels more confident and feminine often has a positive impact on all those around her; her family, her friends and her business associates. This is one of the reasons I love what I do. I make a difference in the life of a woman and that difference then flows out to others.

A woman who feels confident and feminine often has a positive impact on those around her.

Wesley Goes in For a Touch Up

A few months went by and it was time to complete my promise to Wesley. Once again some very generous and gracious people made this happen. Cathy Sullivan, the general Manager of St Vincent's Private Hospital, Kew gave the go ahead for the surgery to be performed at the hospital, for no cost. Dr Andrew Rubinfeld, anaesthetist, Trish McCristal, the best scrub nurse in the world and the rest of the St Vincent's team offered their services free of charge. My colleague Mr Craig Rubinstein agreed to assist and support me with the operation. Colin Smith once again became involved with logistics. Wesley was contacted, Stephen Taylor at *60 Minutes* was contacted and a date was set in early July 2014. As my colleague and now Professor Michael Leung had performed the last operations on Wesley I called him to invite him to the procedure. Unfortunately, he was unable to attend, so we talked about the best way to approach the bulge on Wesley's neck. The last thing I wanted was to damage the blood supply to the flap on Wesley's neck and compromise much of the work that had been done. We felt it best to perform some liposuction to thin the flap out by removing fat and so reduce the width of his neck.

During the filming of the original surgery on Wesley, a reporter for *60 Minutes* had not been appointed. Stephen was already talking about going to PNG to complete the story, so a reporter now needed to be appointed and pick up the story. I was delighted when Stephen told me the reporter would be Karl Stefanovic. I had watched Karl on the *Today* show and he was clearly an exceptional talent.

Prior to the operation, Karl visited Wesley at his workplace with the Salvation Army in Sydney. Karl spent a lot of time getting to know Wes, laughing and joking with him, so that Wes was comfortable in his presence, with the cameras rolling. The day before his operation, Wesley came to my rooms in Melbourne. It was good to see him again. He was laid back, excited to have some more work done and completely nonplussed with the attention he was to receive.

Unfortunately, Stephen was producing another story when the operation was to be performed, however, one of the assistant producers filled in admirably. Wesley and I were filmed as I marked him out in his hospital room. He was relaxed and his main concern was how long before he could eat again.

The operation was scheduled for late in the afternoon to accommodate Karl's busy schedule. By the time the operation was due to start, Karl had not arrived, so we waited. And waited. We had reports that he had actually arrived in Melbourne and was on his way but there was no sign of him. We decided to start the operation and hopefully he would arrive part way through. As Dr Andrew Rubinfeld drifted Wesley off to sleep, the last thing Wes said to me was make sure I preserve his dreadlocks! For this operation, the anaesthetist had no trouble inserting a tube into Wesley's mouth and for me, in spite of the camera and microphone beneath my sterile gown, it was much less stressful than the original procedure. The operation took less than an hour and when we had finished we got word that Karl was almost there. He had gone to the wrong hospital, which just happened to be a mental health facility. Whilst he had brightened the day of staff and patients he had to leave quickly when the patients started screaming and he discovered his error. When Karl eventually arrived, he breezed in, introduced himself, apologised, quickly assessed the situation and took on his professional demeanour. He had done his homework and was well aware of Wesley's journey so far. With the camera rolling, he and I had some back and forth dialogue and then the anaesthetist woke Wesley up. Karl disappeared as quickly as he had arrived and moved to his next appointment. That night he played in the AFL Legend's game and even kicked a goal.

Wesley came through the procedure extremely well. When I saw him the next day he had been awake most of the night watching television and was tucking into a second breakfast. I think he was disappointed I said he could go home because he was enjoying the excellent care he was receiving in the ward. With liposuction, areas that are treated are typically swollen postoperatively and the best results are not seen for three months or longer. However, I was pleased with the early result on his neck and this improved as time went on. More importantly, Wesley was also pleased.

With the success of this procedure, planning for the final part of the story was underway. Allowing time for Wesley's recovery then finding a time when both Karl and I were available for a week, was not easy. The best time seemed to be early in the New Year and I adjusted my schedule to include a trip to PNG with Wesley, Karl and the *60 Minutes* team.

Twenty-Two Years in the Making

In mid January, 2015 Wesley and I travelled to PNG to complete a trip that was 22 years in the making. I arrived at Sydney airport early and introduced myself to a guy who was getting ready to check in a large amount of equipment. It was Chick Davey—The Chickman— who was the Sound Engineer. Andy Taylor, the Cameraman, with an even larger amount of equipment, closely followed him, along with Stephen Taylor, the producer. Each of the team was delivered to the airport by limousine, something that Wesley thought he could get very used to. Karl used his influence to gain access for us to the Qantas Chairman's Lounge. I could get very used to that.

It wasn't long before I witnessed what it was like to be a celebrity, for most places we went, Karl was recognised. In the past, celebrities would sign autographs. Nowadays, everybody wants to have their photograph taken with the celebrity. Each and every time this was requested of Karl, he obliged, with a smile on his face. This was also true in PNG where the *Today* show is screened on local television. Over the next week, Karl was asked for his photograph close on 100 times. I can imagine it would get very tiring to be in the public eye all the time yet he handled it with grace and good humour.

We arrived in Port Moresby and were taken to the hotel where all the staff were lined up, waiting for a photo with Karl. Shortly thereafter we were introduced to the Hon. Justin Tkatchenko MP the Sports Minister in charge of the Pacific Games due to be held later in the year. Justin was very personable and took the whole team out for a delicious dinner at one of the local seafood restaurants. The following morning, the filming commenced as Wes, Karl and I were introduced to the PNG Prime Minister, Hon. Peter O'Neill CMG MP, at his office in Parliament House. For Wesley, this was a special occasion as the Prime Minister acknowledged his courage and commented that he would inspire many in PNG. I thought it was a fitting touch that Wes, a young man from the Eastern Highlands, was the first of all the dignitaries that would sign the visitors book in the Prime Minister's office in 2015.

That afternoon we flew to Goroka, the capital of the Eastern Highlands. Wesley had some of his early treatment at the Goroka Base Hospital following his injury and subsequently attended school there. Consequently, he had some mixed feelings. He looked quite contemplative as he stood on the hill, looking down over the town, a very different person to the terrified little boy who had first arrived more than 20 years previously. Former Eastern Highlands Governor, Malcolm Kela-Smith, hosted us and arranged our transport. Malcolm had been prominent in the area for years, seemed to know everybody, and in a world where things don't tend to happen too quickly, he managed to get things done. Filming was to take place on the hill overlooking Goroka. The dirt road to the summit was never intended for cars and even livestock would have struggled to keep their footing. The intention was to film Wesley in his own environment whilst creating some footage that reflected the traditions and cultures of the ancient land. This was the first time I could really observe the *60 Minutes* team at work. Their teamwork was exceptional led by Stephen Taylor who carried the responsibility for the decisions made. They worked seamlessly together. For sound, Chick would primarily use lapel microphones as well as the boom; Andy would film from different angles with both wide shots and close-ups of faces for maximum impact. His use of the drone to film the Asaro Mudmen stalking their way up the hill, was outstanding. Karl, of course, asked the questions. Karl had done his homework and most impressively, Wesley was relaxed in his company. Karl had spent time getting to know Wes. He joked and laughed with him, yet always had an understanding of the painful journey Wes had undertaken. It is easy to ask questions, but to be emotionally involved in a way that has the interviewee relaxed and open, is a real skill. It was clear to me that Karl has an immense amount of talent.

None of this would have happened without Stephen Taylor's understated leadership. It was important for Stephen that this story go to air in the most respectful and sensitive way possible. It would have been very easy to turn Wesley into a commodity in a cheap grab for ratings. However, a great deal of thought, creativity and professionalism went into how the story was put together. As Karl was asking questions of Wes or I, Stephen would let it run, then ask us to redo a part. He would note the questions and answers and suggest it be asked in a different way or suggest we might like another go at answering. He was invaluable for cutaways where the question or answer needed to be filmed from a different angle. I know this is normal practice with filming, however, I was able to observe its seamlessness with an exceptional team.

Wesley coped with all of this like a true professional. He wasn't intimidated by the microphones or camera and shared his experiences, thoughts and feelings with genuineness and humility. When filming had stopped there were a group of curious and overawed youngsters who had been watching proceedings. Wes went to them, connected with them and had his photo taken with them. I can see that Wes has the potential to inspire many of his own people.

The following day was the pinnacle for Wesley's story. Early in the morning we boarded the helicopter for the 30-minute trip to Wesley's village of Onamuga. This was to be a surprise visit. It had been about ten years since Wes had seen his parents and family and they had no idea he was coming that day. It was Wesley's first trip in a helicopter. He was laid back as usual, however, admitted to some excitement and apprehension about the reception he would receive. He knew his family would be delighted to see him however, it was almost incomprehensible to know that there were some elements in the village who felt he had abandoned them to go off to Australia and make a new life for himself. It was a stunning day and the view from the helicopter of the ancient and rugged PNG terrain was breathtakingly beautiful.

When you arrive by a yellow helicopter in a remote village, it is hard to keep the arrival secret. By the time the chopper blades ceased rotating, hundreds of people had gathered around. Wes and I were miked up and I was asked to accompany him as he left the helicopter and returned to the people of his village for the first time in ten years. News travelled quickly and it was not long before Wes was embraced by his sister, Inomo, then his father, Koni, then his mother, Onampo. In spite of the camera and the hundreds of onlookers, it was a heartwarming time as he was welcomed back to the family. Wesley's father Koni did not appear to have aged one bit. It was 20 years since I had seen him and my lasting memory was of Koni cradling his young son in his arms, protecting him from the cold and inquisitive stares. When he had finished embracing Wes, I said, 'Koni. Hi, it's Malcolm.'

He turned and looked at me, inquisitively, for a few moments. Then it registered who I was.

'Malcolm. Malcolm!', he said excitedly, as he then told his family who I was.

We embraced. The genuine warmth brought tears to my eyes.

I wasn't expecting to be recognised or to be appreciated with such warmth and gratitude. Yet I was being welcomed as part of the family. It was very humbling because I knew I had simply played my role as part of a large team that had made a difference to Wesley. I guess I was the face of that team and Koni was showing his heartfelt appreciation.

As we walked up the hill towards the family residence, Karl was asking me how I felt. I was overwhelmed with the warmth, acceptance and well-wishes of the whole village. I had always known I would be at risk of crying on national television and here I was, not letting anybody down. The camera of course loved it as the close-up shots show. However, not everything was ideal. Firstly, I had developed a stye on my right lower eyelid, which, in spite of antibiotics and warm compresses, seemed to reach its largest size and redness over these few days. Secondly, as I was walking up the hill, a large fly settled on my cheek. Rather than swat it off, I thought seasoned professionals on camera just let them fly off on their own accord. So I left it. Unfortunately, this one seemed to settle in for the duration, which meant there was a big, black fly on my face during some of the most poignant moments of the story. Stephen later told me he had to use some digital expertise during editing and those with a keen eye can pick this up in the footage that went to air.

Some of the most moving moments were spent in the grass hut, similar to the one where Wesley had originally fallen into the fire. The hut is circular with a mud floor and an open fire in the centre. It was easy to see how, if left unattended for a moment, an ill child, could fall into the fire. It was my impression that Wesley's mum had carried this guilt for so long. I suspect my own mother had carried a similar guilt for the injury to my hand. As Wesley, Koni, Onampo, Karl and I sat around the fire, reflecting on what had happened and Wesley's subsequent journey, Koni, with Wesley interpreting, expressed his gratitude to all those who had come together to make a difference to his son.

From the hut, we visited the clinic where Wesley was first taken after he was pulled from the flames. I met some of the nurses who still work there, with limited resources and was amazed that Wes had survived his initial injury. Whilst there, we were shown some of the footage of the original operation. It was a weird experience seeing this for the first time some 22 years later. The memories flooded back; Wesley crying as he was carried into theatre by Dr Bill Shearer the anaesthetist; the challenge with securing his airway; making the initial incisions under local anaesthetic so that a tube could be inserted into his windpipe; being surrounded by a great team with Michael Leung (now Professor) and my sister-in-law Brenda Linsell as scrub nurse; the relief at the end of the operation when things had gone to plan and Wesley was safe. During filming, I made specific mention of these people and others, however, as so often occurs in stories of this nature, the vast majority of the footage is left on the cutting room floor.

Travelling to Wesley's village, meeting his family, appreciating where he had come from, was a deeply moving experience for me.

Very few surgeons have the privilege of retracing a patient's steps over a 20-year period, to fully understand the circumstances surrounding the original accident. As we flew back to Goroka, something had shifted within me. It was a deeper appreciation of the skills that I had been given and the impact these can have, not only on the patient, but on their family and community.

The following day, Malcolm Kela-Smith's house was transformed into a recording studio for the final interviews. Wesley and I were filmed at different times so I had no idea what he had said until it was screened. Karl's skill was evident, as he knew how to draw out emotion. In a one on one interview there is nowhere to hide. Every thought and feeling is potentially exposed. It is the interviewer's role to get down to the real feelings for it is these that connect with the audience. Having been interviewed a few times previously, I was relaxed yet felt vulnerable. For most of the interview I kept my composure, however, was again drawn to tears when I acknowledged I had made a difference in Wesley's life. This is at my core and having been through a challenging period over the previous few years, it was strong validation for me that I was back doing what I love and what I was good at.

*When you love what you do and are very
good at it, it is very rewarding.*

Travelling back home the following day, my ride from the hotel was in the open back of a ute. We finished the day in the Chairman's Lounge and a limousine to home in Sydney. Quite coincidently, at the Goroka Airport, Wesley and I met the Territorial Commanders of the Salvation Army in PNG, Colonel and Mrs Andrew Westrupp. Andrew had heard of Wesley and was delighted to meet him. Not long after the *60 Minutes* program aired, I received an email from

Colonel Westrupp requesting that Wesley and I travel to PNG in 2016 to open the Red Shield Appeal. Wesley jumped at the chance and together we will return to PNG in 2016 for that honour.

Love Actually

Coinciding with my re-entrance to medicine, I re-entered the dating game. After some initial experiences with online dating, I took myself offline whilst I was recovering from my health scare and making arrangements to re-enter medicine. Towards the end of 2013, a mutual friend introduced me to an attractive mother with three children. I enjoyed dating for a few months, however, she ended the relationship early in 2014 essentially because at that stage, I didn't have enough money. I was sad about that, however, understood her concerns because at that stage I was just scraping by.

With all the travel I do, I spend a great deal of time in airport lounges. I still believe that becoming a member of the Qantas Club 20 years previously was one of the best investments I have ever made. On one occasion, I was in the Qantas Club in Melbourne waiting for my flight to Sydney and reading the sports section in the newspaper when I saw an advertisement for elitesingles.com.au. This was an online dating service for genuine single professionals and so-called 'intelligent matchmaking'. That appealed to me as well as did the fact that people paid money up-front, then the site matched applicants on their behalf.

I registered on the EliteSingles site and was matched with several women, some of whom I contacted. I began to see a lovely woman, whom I will call Anna, who was a previous headmistress of a school. A week later, while I was working in Mackay, Dr Kim Amanda Carr, a dentist of 35 years in Double Bay, Sydney, saw an advertisement for EliteSingles whilst watching television at home. Having no experience of online dating, she was nonetheless curious and thought she might check out some of the available talent. She was somewhat irritated to discover that it was not like shopping online at Net-a-Porter. She was required to register and fill out a long application form, which she did—as Amanda, 55 years old, living in Double Bay. She and I were instantly matched. I immediately made contact with 'Amanda' via the site and we exchanged telephone numbers. We exchanged texts for a little while before I asked if I could give her a call. As it was late, we only spoke briefly and I promised to call her the following day when I arrived back into Sydney. She did, however, admit that her real name was Kim and that Amanda was her middle name. I called from the platform of Sydney's Central station the following evening and we arranged to meet for lunch the following day, Saturday, after she had finished work. Meanwhile she Googled my name to see that I was who I said I was and was not an axe murderer.

We met for lunch at Perron's in Double Bay on Saturday 22 February 2014. She breezed into the restaurant and I was taken with her glamour, her intelligence and her humour. She was confident and totally at ease with herself. We talked easily about numerous topics, books we had read, we laughed and had fun. She had the chicken salad and I had nachos. She asked if I was going back to my wife (at that time I had been separated for 17 months). There is conjecture about my answer. I said, 'The chances of me going back to my wife are extremely small.' She heard, 'Yes, it is highly likely I will go back to my wife.'

Regardless, I wanted to see her again. She was out to dinner that night with girlfriends and had brunch booked the following morning. I said I would call her after brunch. That night at dinner, Kim told her girlfriends she had met a guy at lunch, whom she might like. One of the women present, Elizabeth Robinson, has a psychic gift and said 'Yes, I can see it. There is a lot of water between you two and you will get married!'

Kim replied, 'Don't be ridiculous, I am never getting married again!' And the conversation moved on.

What Kim didn't know was that at the time, I lived on the water at McMahon's Point. She lived on the water at Rose Bay. The only thing that separated us was water.

The next morning, Kim checked her emails and was inundated with matches from EliteSingles. She thought she might need to hire an executive assistant to manage the requests, concluded this would be too hard, and promptly deregistered herself from the site. Her total online dating experience lasted eight hours. I was the first and only match to whom she responded.

I called later that morning and arranged to meet her for a drink in the afternoon. Again we had fun chatting and the time passed quickly. We could see her home from the restaurant and I said I would like to visit her place at some time. I was flying to Melbourne that evening so she invited me to her place for dinner the following Friday night when I arrived back from Melbourne. The staff in my Melbourne rooms told me the fact I had been invited to her home for dinner, was a very good sign

I was so excited and couldn't wait for Friday to come around. At lunch the first time we met, one of the things we had discussed was the book, *The Five Love Languages* by Garry Chapman. Kim had shared that her primary love language was gifts, so when I arrived at her place on Friday, I was bearing roses and sweets that she said she liked.

As Kim and I spent more time together, our relationship and friendship grew. Our time together was limited because Monday to Friday I worked in either Melbourne or Queensland, so we made use of our time on the weekends. We went to the Comedy Club for stand up comedy, to the movies, to plays and to lunch and dinner. I loved spending time with her and was amazed with her intelligence, her insight, her intuition, her wit. Her values of doing the right thing, integrity, honesty, compassion, aligned with mine and I felt so privileged to be in relationship with her. And we laughed and laughed. It was rare for a conversation to not include laughter, either about something that occurred that day or about something we had done or said.

In the initial stages of our relationship, Kim was reluctant to meet Bek and Tim. She was appalled that I had introduced other girlfriends to them so early and did not want to intrude as our family was still muddling our way through separation and the inevitable divorce. Every week Bek, Tim and I would go out for breakfast on a Saturday or Sunday morning and they became aware that I was very keen on the dentist from Double Bay. The fact that I didn't come home on weekends and that I had become very, very happy was also a slight giveaway. Kim finally met Bek and Tim a couple of months after we had first met and they knew very early on Kim was right for me. About the same time, I met Michael and India, Kim's children. All of us not only got on, we actually liked each other. That Michael and India are two outstanding young adults is a tribute not only to them, but to Kim who raised them primarily as a single mother.

As a potential suitor for Kim, there was another hurdle for me to overcome—meeting her parents. Dr Ian and Mrs Holly Walters are a formidable couple. He, a former dentist and she, a former nurse are both in their mid eighties, are fit, healthy and as sharp as two tacks. Along with Kim, Michael and India, I was invited to a Walters family dinner, where I was to experience some of Holly's excellent hospitality. Just as I was beginning to feel comfortable, Dr Walters produced my personal examination paper. A hush descended upon the dinner table, which for a Walter's family dinner is a rarity. I was then put through one of the most gruelling oral examinations I have ever faced. My understanding is that I just scraped through with a score of nine out of ten, however, the answer to one of the questions is still in dispute for I still think that AFL is the better game!

I was dating the most beautiful, intelligent, confident, glamorous woman I could imagine. Kim and her daughter, India, had travelled to Melbourne to watch me in the operating theatre. India was considering training in either dentistry or medicine so, just as another plastic surgeon had done for me 40 years previously, I invited her to theatre to observe. Kim just wanted to see me at work. This is the first time she had met our theatre team, Drs Craig Rubinstein and Andrew Rubinfeld along with Trish McCristal. When Kim and India had left the theatre, Craig said to me, 'Well, she's a keeper. Don't let her go!'

Early in our relationship, Kim told me about a cruise around the Mediterranean, she had booked for July. I invited myself along. I had no doubt we would get along. Kim had a backup plan just in case. It is one thing to see each other on weekends. It is another to spend every minute of every day together for two weeks in an enclosed environment. However, we had such fun. Kim spent the first week of her holiday dancing on the tables at St Tropez so that by the time we met in Rome, she was already relaxed. This was my first cruise and because I spend so much time travelling, to be visiting places such as Corsica, to have mussels on the water's edge, to have afternoon tea overlooking the breathtaking beauty of Portofino or exploring the magnificence of Gaudi architecture in Barcelona, without having to unpack my suitcase, was a sheer delight. During this trip, I discovered that when Kim shops, she shops! The inside of a designer store seemed to be as familiar to her as the inside of a dental surgery. Fortuitously, there happened to be a Tiffany's in Barcelona, which I thought might be interesting to check out. Whilst she showed some initial resistance, as soon as she was inside she got with the program very quickly. She tried on a few rings and the one she really liked was a Tiffany 'Soleste'. I filed this away in my memory banks for later reference.

We were fortunate to spend Christmas and New Year in Hawaii and I was the happiest I had been for many years. I remember arriving at the hotel and watching the sunset over the Pacific Ocean. It had been less than 18 months since I had been at my lowest ebb and now I was in one of the most magical places on earth, with the most beautiful woman in the world and my career was starting to grow and grow. With some smart decisions and surrounding myself with some good people, my personal turnaround was occurring very rapidly. I felt very blessed. There just happened to be a Tiffany's in Waikiki as well. Kim feigned reluctance, however, she was again drawn to the 'Soleste', which seemed to be increasing in price every time we looked.

New year 2015 dawned with more excitement and optimism that I had had for many years.

Good decisions and good people can
help change the circumstances of life can
change very quickly.

The *60 Minutes* program, entitled Wesley's Homecoming, was screened on Sunday 10 May 2015, Mother's Day in Australia. Stephen called me at the beginning of the week to let me know it would be on. I had not seen any of the footage, nor had any say over the content, so whilst I felt excited, I also had some anxiety as I was unsure how either Wes or I would be portrayed. It felt quite surreal watching *The Footy Show* in Melbourne on the Thursday night and then seeing the promos for the story. Friends immediately started texting me and it was a weird sensation observing both Wes and I, trying to be objective, whilst thinking we both scrubbed up okay.

The Sunday night it screened, I was flying to Melbourne on the last flight out of Sydney. I was watching with Kim, Bek, Tim and India along with Michael, my driver, and could not have been more pleased with how the story was portrayed. My children, always a great leveller, have never allowed me to forget that I cried on national television and there is now a photograph in the home, capturing that moment, stye and all, forever. As I travelled to the airport, then boarded QF497, I was stunned with the public response, particularly on the *60 Minutes* Facebook page. I was deeply touched and profoundly humbled with the comments.

The response was so strong, that Stephen asked Wes and I to meet again so that some follow-up footage could be filmed, to be screened the following week. I flew up from Melbourne for a few hours and it was like a family reunion to see Wes, Stephen, Andy and Chick again.

I found the whole experience with *60 Minutes* to be immensely satisfying. Television is a very powerful medium and can be used at a director's whim to portray individuals in a positive or negative light. At all times the *60 Minutes* team were respectful of Wesley and his family, professional in their approach and genuine in their desire to tell a story of a young boy's incredible courage in overcoming and moving beyond adversity. Wesley inspires me. If I inspire others as well, I can't think of anything I would rather be doing.

My relationship with Kim deepened after the *60 Minutes* program. In spite of her highly successful career, her success in marriage had been less than optimal. Marriage for me is the ultimate expression of a relationship. It is a lifelong commitment of two people to be faithful to each other no matter what. I knew I wanted to be married to Kim for the rest of my life. A marriage proposal is not something a man takes lightly. It takes a lot of courage and often a lot of preparation. It is a question he only expects to make once in his lifetime and he expects the answer to be in the affirmative. If not, why would he bother asking? I had made Kim aware that if I ever did ask her to marry me, I would only be asking once.

In mid 2014, whilst in Melbourne together, we just happened to find ourselves in Tiffany's at Chadstone. Yes, there was a pattern here and I was noticing considerably less reluctance from Kim when viewing some of the options. A short time later, I was consulting in my Melbourne rooms, when I received a call with a Sydney number. I answered.

'Hello, Dr Linsell. It's Kylie from Tiffany's in Sydney here.'

'Yes', I said, quite suspiciously.

'I am with your girlfriend, Dr Carr, and she has chosen the ring.'

'Oh, has she?' I said, even more suspiciously.

'Yes. And quite amazingly, the only place the ring is available in the southern hemisphere is in our Melbourne showroom.'

'Really?' I said. 'How very convenient.'

'Yes,' she said. 'I have set the ring aside for you so if you want to pop in over the next few days, my colleagues in Melbourne will be happy to show it to you.'

'I'm sure they will,' I said. 'Thank-you for letting me know.'

I hung up and laughed. That was Kim. If I was going to propose, she wanted to make sure I produced the right ring, rather than one she didn't like but had to make out she did.

I didn't mention the conversation to Kim. I didn't want her to know if I had done anything further for I wanted the timing and the circumstances to be a surprise. A few days later I had a morning operating list in a hospital close to Melbourne's CBD. After the list I drove to Tiffany's in Melbourne and indeed found the ring that had been set aside. It was the 'Soleste' and it was beautiful. I knew Kim would love it. Once I have decided to do something I make a plan and follow through. We were due to go to Europe for a plastic surgical conference in a few months and I was considering proposing whilst I was there. A week or so later, I returned to Tiffany's and purchased the ring. I was excited and happy, though as I was leaving the Tiffany's consultant told me the money-back guarantee was only for 30 days. That meant Europe was not an option and I needed an alternate plan. Earlier that week, Kim had called to say the restaurant in the Sydney Opera House, Bennelong, had reopened and she had booked a table for us on Saturday evening. It occurred to me that as Kim had made the booking, she would be unsuspecting that I was up to anything.

I arrived back in Sydney on Friday 3 July 2015 and as my driver Michael Zacccariou, was driving me to Rose Bay, I noticed it was a full moon. I decided then and there that the following evening I would ask Kim to marry me. Michael had been driving me for most of the time I had been back in plastic surgery. On one occasion, I had used an Uber and had been impressed with the driver's care, service and energy. I asked for his card and Michael had been driving me ever since. When Michael dropped me off, I asked him to pick us up the following night to take us to the Opera House.

Saturday 4 July 2015 in Sydney was cold by our standards. It was just as well because a Tiffany box is quite bulky and doesn't easily fit into a pants pocket without drawing attention to itself. My overcoat, however, disguised it very well. I was concerned it would be obvious when my coat was taken at the restaurant. I needn't have worried. Kim led the way to the table, and as I followed her she was completely oblivious to the bulge near my right hip.

After two fabulous courses, the Tiffany's box was transferred from my pocket into my lap. The moon was in the perfect spot. Kim's favourite dessert is pavlova and this had been ordered for dessert. I was just about to ask the question, when dessert arrived unexpectedly. At the Bennelong the meringue of the pavlova is in the shape of the Opera House sails. It is spectacular. Kim loved it and of course wanted to take a photo. This included one of myself trying to look composed. By now the box felt like it was burning a hole in my lap but I had to wait while the photo was taken and then of course posted on Facebook. For tech savvy young people this is a breeze. For more mature people like ourselves, this takes a little more energy.

With the Facebook post successfully uploaded, Kim picked up her spoon to commence her dessert.

'Just before you do,' I said, 'there is something I would like to run by you.'

'Okay,' she said, a little inquisitively.

With that, I got down on one knee, told her that she was the smartest, most beautiful woman I had ever had the privilege of meeting and I would be honoured if we could spend the rest of our lives together.

'Kim, will you marry me?' I asked, a little tearily.

'Yes,' she said, between her own tears.

With that I produced the gift-wrapped Tiffany box and when she had opened it, I placed the ring on her left ring finger.

We were both very, very happy. It must have showed because shortly thereafter our waiter came back to the table.

'Oh, it looks like something special has happened here.' he said.

'Yes,' I responded. 'We have just got engaged.'

'Oh wonderful. Congratulations. Can I see the ring?' Kim held out her left hand for him to view.

'Oh dear. I am so jealous!' he exclaimed.

I wasn't sure if he was jealous of Kim, me, the ring or something else. Nevertheless, he was very excited for us.

Just at that moment, the fireworks from Darling Harbour commenced. These are a regular occurrence at 9pm on a Saturday night, however, for us the timing was perfect. The restaurant offered us champagne to celebrate and one of the waiters took our photograph with the Sydney Harbour Bridge in the background.

*A proposal for marriage is one of the
most important questions a person
will ever ask, so give it some thought
and preparation.*

Our driver, Michael was the first to know. I wanted to speak with Kim's parents, who lived not far away, however, it was a little late. That would wait until the morning.

When morning broke, I was intending to call Kim's parents, however, we decided it would be better if we visited them a little later. Before I told anybody else, I thought the right thing to do was to let my former wife Fiona know. This I did by email. Next I wanted to call my children and was aware I needed to be very sensitive to them. I called Bek who was so excited and happy for me. I then called Tim and whilst he was happy for me, I suspect for him, it was the final confirmation that his mum and I would never be back together. I think times like this are very difficult for children no matter how old they are or how well adjusted they might appear. We invited all our children around for pizza that Sunday night. They all came, they were all happy and we had a lot of fun celebrating as a family for the first time.

*In divorce, it is the children who are most
impacted so at all times be respectful and
sensitive to how they might be feeling.*

In spite of my age, I felt it was the right thing to do to seek permission from Kim's parents. On Sunday morning we both went to their apartment and I had prepared a few things to say. Holly answered the door and before I could say anything, Kim flashed her left hand out and excitedly exclaimed, 'We're engaged!' Her Mum appeared delighted, though we had to wait several hours to speak with Ian as he was out playing golf. He was also very happy for us both and from the beginning I felt accepted and my children were accepted, into the Walters family.

It was not difficult to come up with the idea for a destination wedding. We wanted our wedding to be small with family and a few friends. I had never been to Hayman Island, however, Kim had been often and many of her friends had raved about the major refurbishment performed by the 'One and Only' brand. We chose Hayman Island and when word began to get out, people started inviting themselves.

We chose Sunday 29 November 2015 for our wedding. To me, once you have decided to marry, it's better to marry earlier rather than later, particularly when you are our age. About six weeks prior to the wedding, we travelled to Hayman Island to better appreciate the logistics as well as taste the food and wine. Everything was excellent, including our wedding coordinator, Stephanie New, who left nothing to chance. The only slight problem was that it rained the whole weekend. We were assured the chances of this in late November were remote. Nevertheless, it gave Kim something extra to be slightly stressed about.

A Perfect Wedding

We wanted our wedding to be simple, meaningful, enjoyable and fun for all. We are fortunate that we each have two children and each have a boy and a girl. The fact they are outstanding individuals and appear to like each other is an added bonus. We wanted our children to make up our bridal party and we were delighted when they each jumped at the chance. Kim's niece,

Maddy, had been her flower girl at her prior wedding. India had been the flower girl at Maddy's wedding. Maddy's daughter, Lily, was asked to be the flower girl at our wedding. She was so excited. I had known Major Bryce and Major Sue Davies from the Salvation Army, all of their lives. When we were younger, Bryce and I had played together in the Camberwell Salvation Army Band and a smaller group known as Jubilant Brass. We had also spent many hours thrashing out various aspects of faith in a Bible Study held at 11pm on a Friday night. Bryce was now working for the Army on the streets of Brisbane and as a fully ordained Salvation Army officer he had done many weddings. Kim and I thought it would add a special touch to have someone that knew me well, to marry us. Bryce and Sue were delighted to be asked and made sure we had all the documentation complete.

With a bit of help from the internet, we composed our own vows. Kim's friend, Louise McBride, agreed to read and my brother, Derek Linsell, agreed to pray. I wanted a hymn. Kim wasn't so sure because hymns at weddings are not that common nowadays. We found a version of 'O Perfect Love' that would work. This hymn is more a prayer from the audience to the bride and groom, 'that theirs might be the love that knows no ending.' Just to be sure some would sing I sent several people the link to the song as well as the lyrics so there were no excuses.

Kim had her dress designed and made by Alex Perry. He asked her if she wanted to be 'comfortable or thin?'

'Why, thin of course!' was her reply.

The chapel on Hayman Island is on the hill, with a panoramic view of the ocean. Tim, Michael and myself arrived early, made sure the music was set up and then greeted all the guests. We had plenty of time as Kim was 30 minutes late. Just as we were considering looping the music for the third time, the white Rolls Royce arrived. This was the signal to play Kim's choices, a couple of Meghan Trainor hits. The first was 'Dear Future Husband' which brought a few smiles to the congregation. Then the rear doors opened and the bridal party entered to 'Like I'm Gonna Lose You'. First Lily, then Bek then India. Each of the girls were stunning. Then I had my first glimpse of Kim and she took my breath away. She looked radiant, so beautiful, in a dress that was perfect for her, proudly escorted down the aisle by her father, Dr Ian Walters. At that moment, I felt like the luckiest man in the world.

The service was simple and intimate. The highlight was the vows. As I commenced, my voice was breaking, but as I looked into Kim's eyes, I said and meant every word.

'I, Malcolm David Linsell take you, Kim Amanda Carr, to be my wife, my constant friend, and my love from this day forward. In the presence of God, our family and friends, I offer you my solemn vow to be your faithful partner in sickness and in health, for richer for poorer, in good times and in bad, and in joy as well as in sorrow.

'I love and adore you and want nothing more than to share my future with you.

'I promise to love you unconditionally, to support you in your goals, to honour and respect you, to laugh with you and cry with you, and to cherish you for as long as we both shall live. Together, I know we can accomplish the life we both dream of living.'

Kim's vows were almost identical.

To us, this was a sacred moment. Speaking these words to each other, in the presence of God, our family and friends is the sealing of a lifelong commitment. In a world where instant gratification is king, we were saying we will be there for each other, forever, irrespective of the circumstances.

It is deeply humbling that another loves me so much, that they are willing to make that commitment. That she is my perfect princess, makes me feel like the happiest man on this planet.

Part Seven

What I have Learned About Myself

Heritage

There is a famous line in the Eagles great hit, 'Hotel California', which says, 'You can checkout any time you like, but you can never leave!' It is also true of the Salvation Army. The values of honesty, integrity, compassion, trustworthiness and respect are deeply ingrained in the Army and are deeply ingrained in me. My grandparents and my mum and dad lived these values so I was privileged to witness them in action, first hand. My mum and dad wanted to make a difference in people's lives through their calling to the Christian ministry. Early on, I also wanted to make a difference and felt that medicine was the best avenue for this.

The Salvation Army is also a culture of faith and respect for authority. The overwhelming majority of people in the organisation are trustworthy. I grew up not having to or needing to question. I naively trusted that those in authority had my best interests at heart.

Plastic Surgery, Then

I was born with some intelligence and talent. Along the way I became egotistical and occasionally narcissistic, which was a front for insecurity. Plastic surgery was an ideal profession for me. Having been well-trained, I could use the skill with my hands to make a difference, get well paid for it and have status in the community.

My practice quickly became successful and I was good at what I did. I enjoyed the impact my surgery had on the way my patients felt about themselves. For a young surgeon, taking on Wesley was a major challenge, yet was immensely rewarding because it gave him a chance to live a normal life.

My values went askew when I began to focus on money rather than people. I took the privilege of medicine for granted and my ego had me believing that because I was a successful doctor, I could be successful in business, particularly if it was designed to make a difference in more people's lives.

Lessons in Business and Life

My desire to be a better person led me into attending courses run by several personal development organisations. As I was gaining insight into my own behaviour, I discovered an organisation run by two charismatic people, who appeared trustworthy, and had a similar but larger vision to mine with a plan to achieve it. After much (but not enough) discussion with my wife, we invested in the organisation and I left medicine to work with and for a company based in Singapore. We were not to know it at the time, however, I now believe this organisation to be a commercial cult. The business was legitimate, however, the vast majority of funds raised by various companies found their way to the two founders. Meanwhile, the good people who worked for the organisation continued to work on behalf of their clients, at great cost to themselves and their personal relationships. Several became bankrupt. Those that didn't, lost all their money. Of those that stayed, eight marriages, five with children ended in divorce. Not one marriage or long-term relationship survived. Sadly, my marriage was one of the casualties.

I am an intelligent person, with strong values, a supportive family and friends. How did I allow this to happen?

Simple. I believed in the company's vision to add value to many people. Furthermore, I believed this would be hugely profitable for our investors and for my family. My primary mistake was to trust in people who were untrustworthy.

If I had my time again I would:

- Do my due diligence on the founders and the organisation.
- Set limits and cut my financial losses early.
- Have back up plans for when plan A is clearly not working.
- Seek advice from independent experts often.
- Continually check-in with my wife and my family.
- Not offer the opportunity to invest to friends.

As a direct result of this experience, we lost our money, my marriage broke down and I had a major health challenge. It took that much for me to wake up to myself. When I did, what hadn't changed were my core values and in particular the desire to do the right thing, my love for my children and my resilience.

I can be beaten and broken but I will learn from the experience and come back a humbler, yet way more powerful person.

Relationships

I firmly believe that a commitment to being lifelong faithful partners in marriage is the ideal for intimate human relationships. It is best for both the children and the individuals making the commitment. A breakdown in this relationship and the mistrust that ensues, leads to hurt for all parties that rarely completely heals perfectly. When someone is physically burned, the body heals with scar tissue, however, as Wesley and my stories demonstrate, function is limited and the scar tissue behaves differently to normal skin. When my marriage broke down, my heart and my children's hearts were lacerated. Our hearts have healed with scar tissue. The resilience of Bek and Tim has been astonishing and yet I suspect the three of us will always carry a little sadness and hurt with us. Is this a bad thing? I don't think so for the human heart is adaptable and has the capacity to grow when we have the courage to embrace others and be open to love again. With my own personal experiences, I have become a more empathic, compassionate and less judgemental person than I was before.

To love again requires trust in the person we are choosing to love and most importantly, trust in ourselves. If we can trust ourselves to be faithful and kind, then no matter what happens, we can always find a way through difficulty and always hold our head high.

The Future

This is the best time of my life. I have just married a woman that I know is perfect for me. We spent the first few days of our honeymoon surrounded by our children and family. I couldn't have wished this to be better. My immediate family has increased in size and I am so proud to be a father with four children. I am having fun, love being married to Kim and am so excited for my future.

My plastic surgical practice is expanding. I have no plans to retire and will continue to work as long as I can continue to add value. As well as my work in Melbourne, Rockhampton and Cairns, I plan to practise in Sydney in 2016, offering a bespoke service for every patient, whether they have skin cancer or are requesting a cosmetic procedure. Every person has the right to feel good about themselves. If I can contribute to that process, my life is truly blessed.

Postscript

Not long ago a woman posted on my plastic surgery Facebook page. Her name was Karen Hawkins. The last time I had spoken with Karen was almost 20 years previously. At that time, she was married to Scott, had a three-year-old boy and was 15-weeks pregnant. I referred her for surgical treatment of a melanoma of the scalp with the distinct possibility she and her unborn child would not survive. Twenty years later, Karen and Scott came to my surgery and it was a sheer delight to see them both. Karen had survived her melanoma and she now had a 23-year-old son, Mitch and a 19-year-old daughter Tayla. Tayla was the daughter she might never have had. Karen just wanted to see me and to say thank you for being so supportive when she had to make some very difficult decisions as to whether or not she kept her unborn child. I had no idea I had made a difference in Karen and her family's life. I was deeply moved.

Two days before Christmas, 2015, I had lunch with Wesley, Stephen Taylor and Andy Taylor from *60 Minutes*. Chick Davey and Karl Stefanovic sent their apologies as they were away. Stephen and Andy said they rarely catch up with people from their stories so it was good to see them. We chatted, laughed, told stories and had fun. Wesley is doing well. He occasionally gets recognised as 'that boy from the TV.' One woman walked up to him and without introduction, gave him a hug. Stephen suggested he must be very special because 'we don't get hugs'. Wes is enjoying life, still working for the Salvos and looking forward to next year. In other words, he is living a 'normal' life. Later, by SMS, he thanked me for an awesome day. Wesley, you are the one who made my day awesome.

To Karen, Wesley and many, many others, you are the ones who have contributed to the life of an ordinary man and made it into something extraordinary.

Acknowledgements

Following the screening of the *60 Minutes* story entitled 'Wesley's Homecoming' I was contacted by Diane Ward from New Holland Publishing, enquiring if I would be interested in writing a book. I had always wanted to write, however, I wasn't sure if the timing was right or even if my life's story would be of interest. Diane assured me there would be interest, particularly if I was open and honest. This book would not be in existence without Diane's encouragement and suggestions. For the opportunity to share my life's experiences in this way, I am very grateful to Diane and New Holland.

Thank you to those whose photographs have been used in this book. In particular, a thank-you to Frank Groeneveld for his comprehensive pre and postoperative shots of Wesley, to Stephen Taylor for allowing us to use many of his brilliant shots in PNG and to Parker Blain for his creative shots of the wedding. Thanks also to Andy Taylor and Jo Bursill for capturing the author on a good day.

The written word is not Wesley's preferred method of communicating, unless it is a short update on his Facebook site. He is more adept with photography or drawing. I am privileged that he readily agreed to write a Foreword. Wes, thank you for this, and for allowing me to be part of your life for more than 20 years. May our connection continue for many years into the future.

My sister, Denise Waterworth, my sister-in-law, Tracy Davis and my friend Michelle Kearney were the first to read the manuscript. For their insightful comments and support, when I wasn't sure if it would resonate with anybody, I am particularly grateful.

Our children, Rebekah and Timothy Linsell, and Michael and India Carr, have been supportive from the beginning. Bek, Tim and

241

I have shared the worst and best of circumstances. Sharing some of these experiences is not easy for them, however, they allowed me to write without restriction. All four of our children are compassionate and well adjusted adults. I could not be more proud of them.

To my wife Kim, 'that book' is now complete. It would not have happened without your support, encouragement and willingness to listen and critique various pieces. Thank you. I am honoured to be your husband and partner for life.

First published in 2016 by New Holland Publishers Pty Ltd
London • Sydney • Auckland

The Chandlery, Unit 704, 50 Westminster Bridge Road, London, SE1 7QY, United Kingdom
1/66 Gibbes Street, Chatswood, NSW, 2067, Australia
5/39 Woodside Avenue, Northcote, Auckland, 0627, New Zealand

www.newhollandpublishers.com

A record of this book is held at the British Library and the National Library of Australia.

ISBN 9781742578675

Managing Director: Fiona Schultz
Publisher: Diane Ward
Project Editor: Liz Hardy
Design: Thomas Partridge
Cover Photography: Sue Stubbs
Production Director: James Mills-Hicks
Printer: Toppan Leefung Printing Limited

10 9 8 7 6 5 4 3 2 1

Keep up with New Holland Publishers on Facebook
www.facebook.com/NewHollandPublishers

AN ORDINARY MAN,

2